Travel

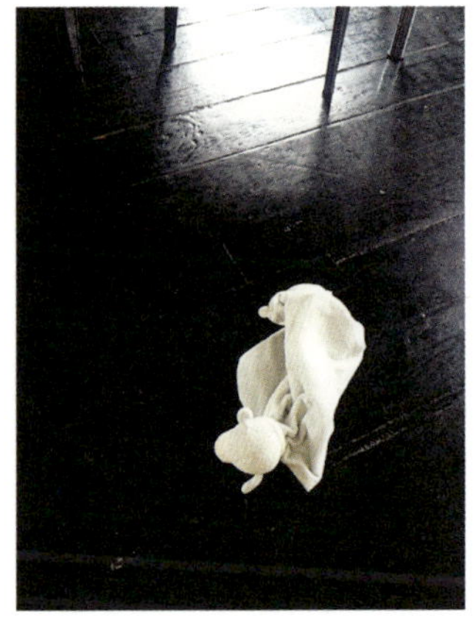

Haim Steinbach   Travel

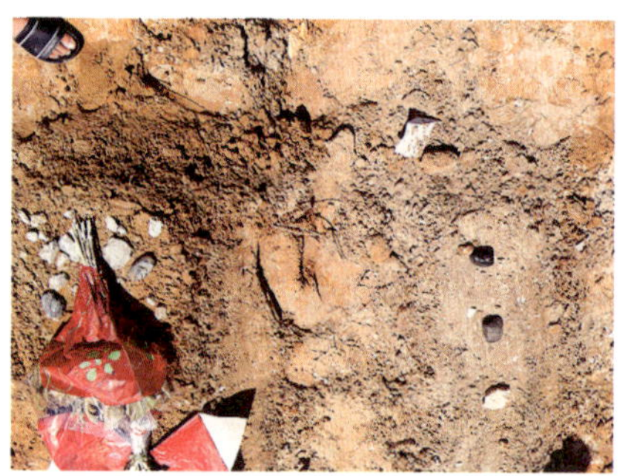

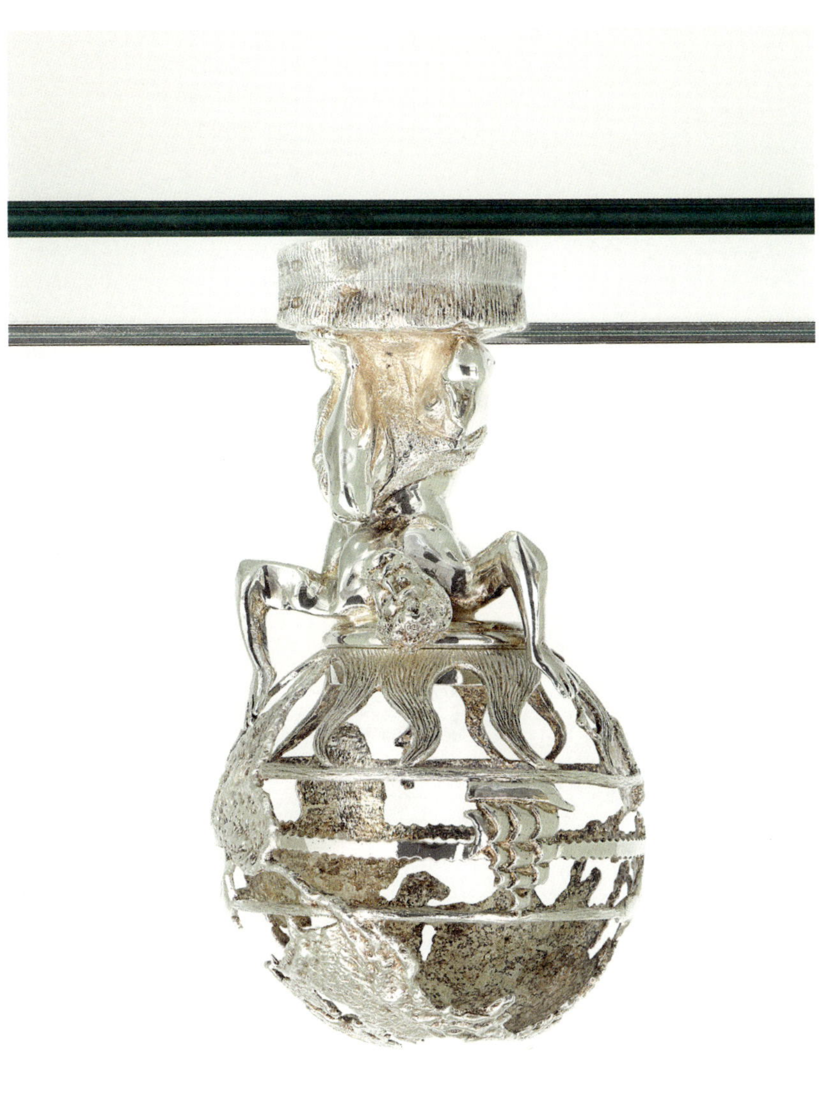

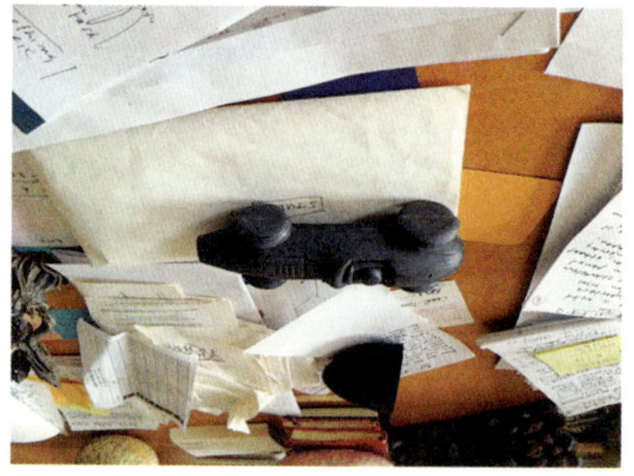

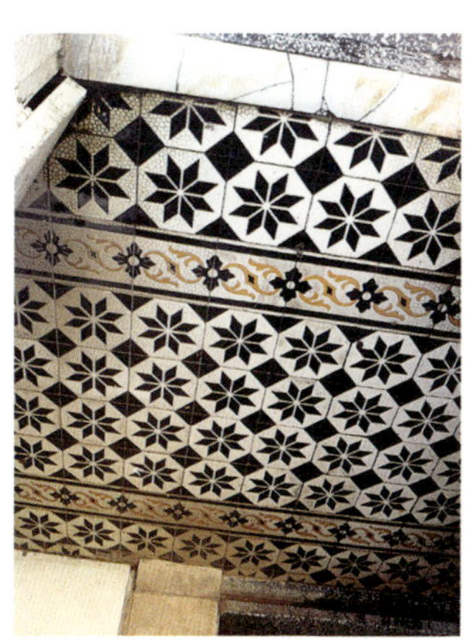

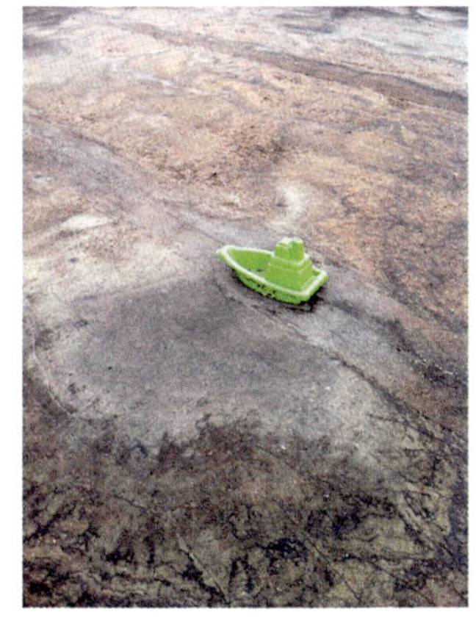

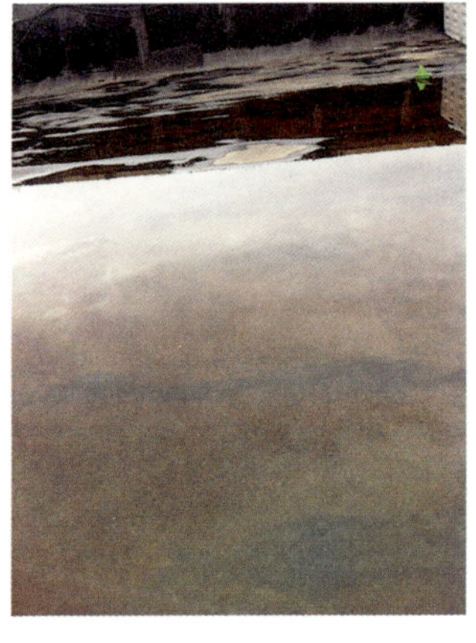

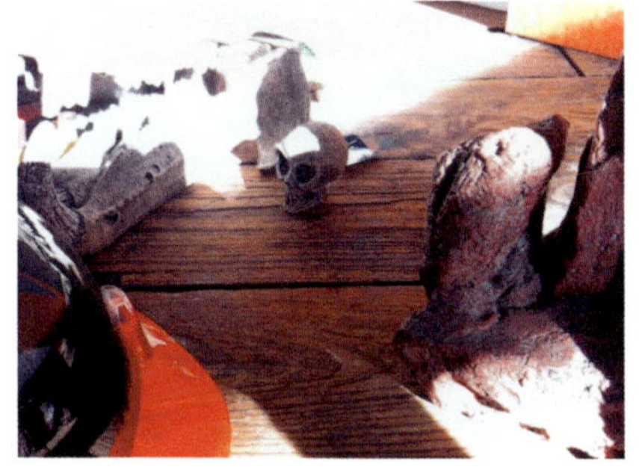

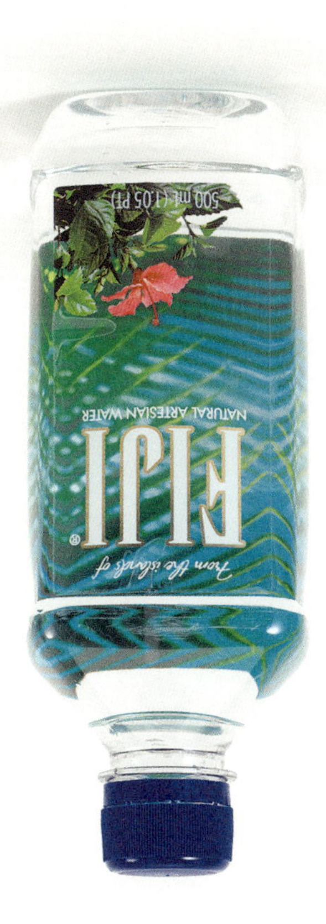

500 mL (1.05 PT)
NATURAL ARTESIAN WATER
From the islands of
FIJI

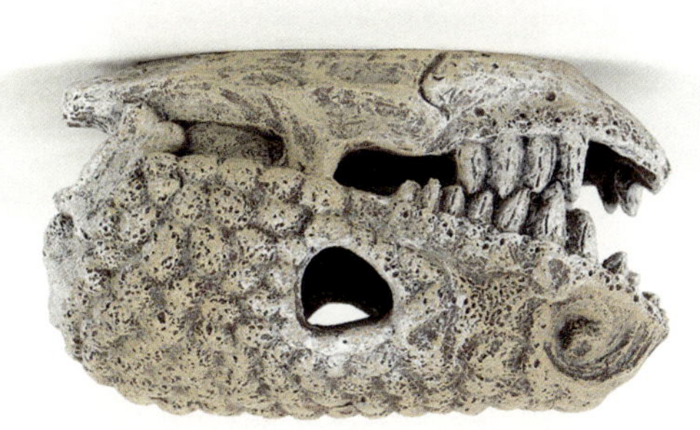

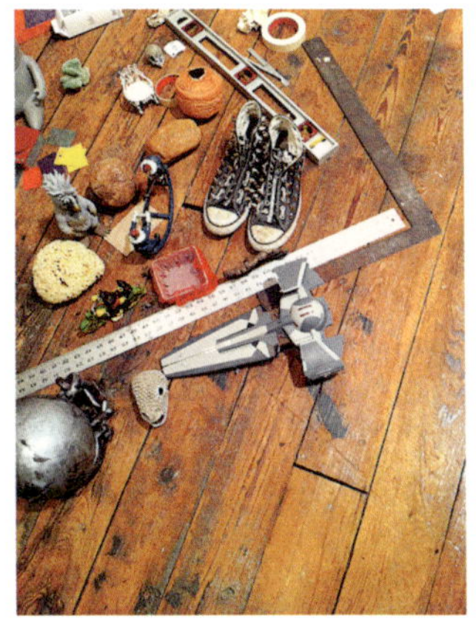

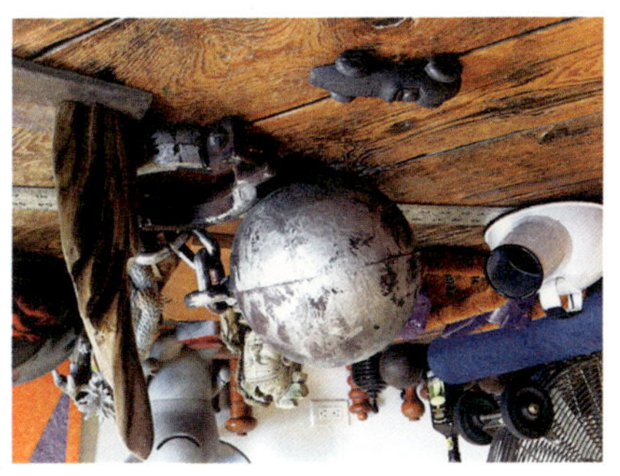

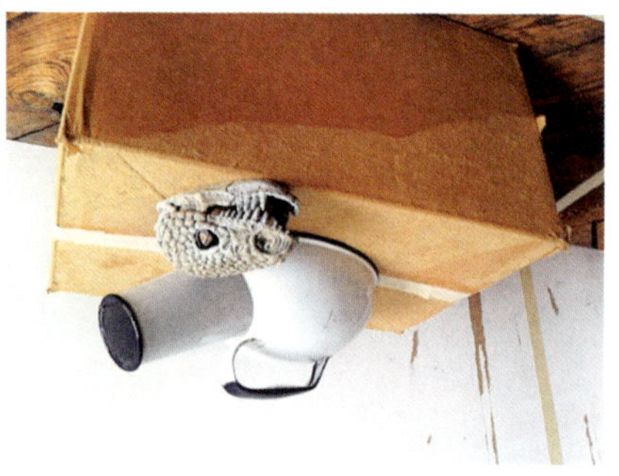

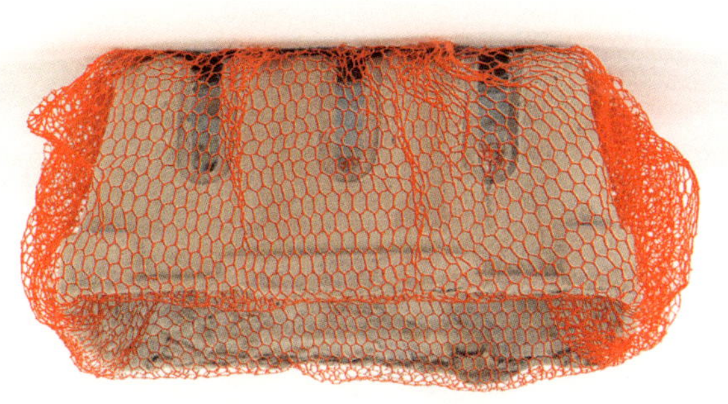

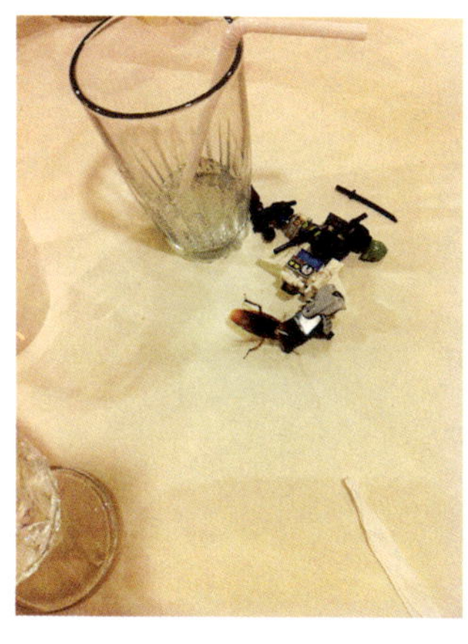

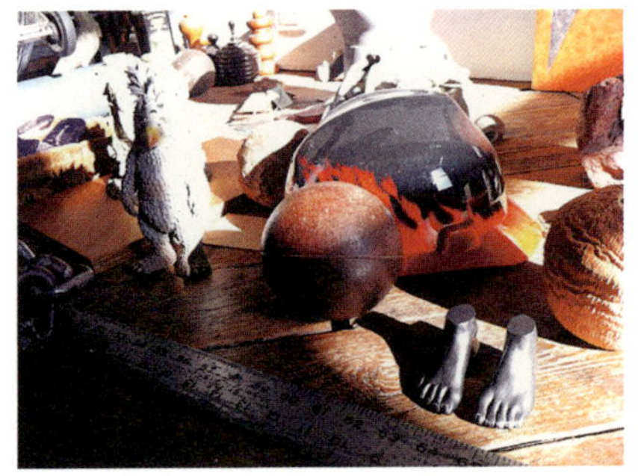

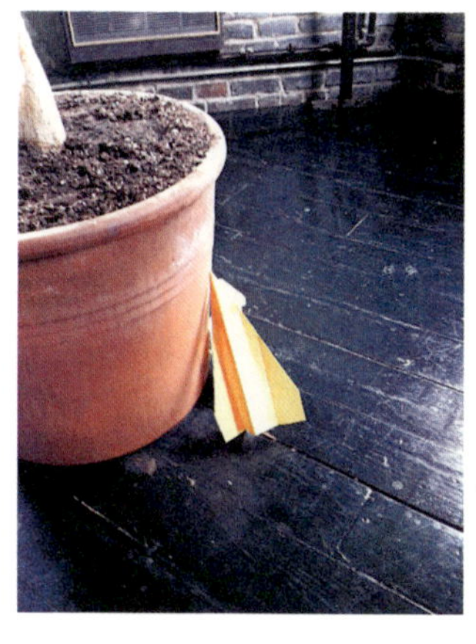

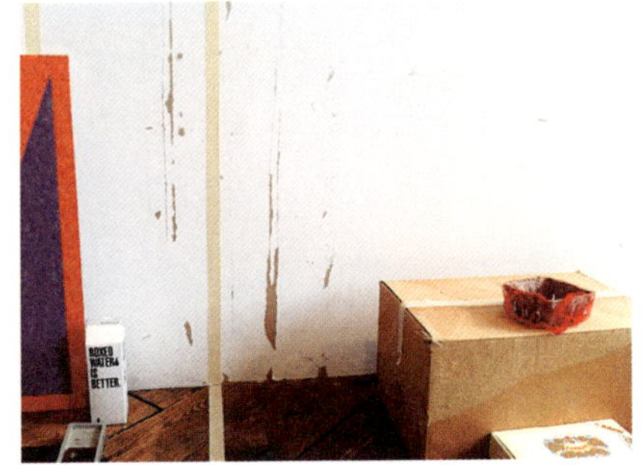

BOXED
WATER
IS
BETTER.

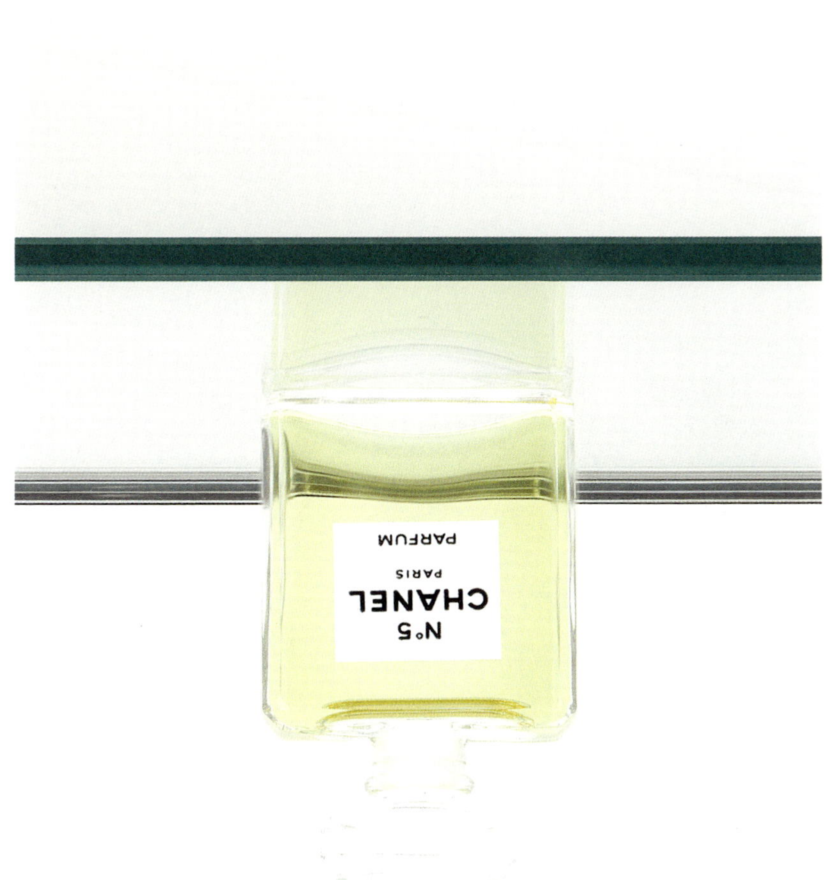

N°5
CHANEL
PARIS
PARFUM

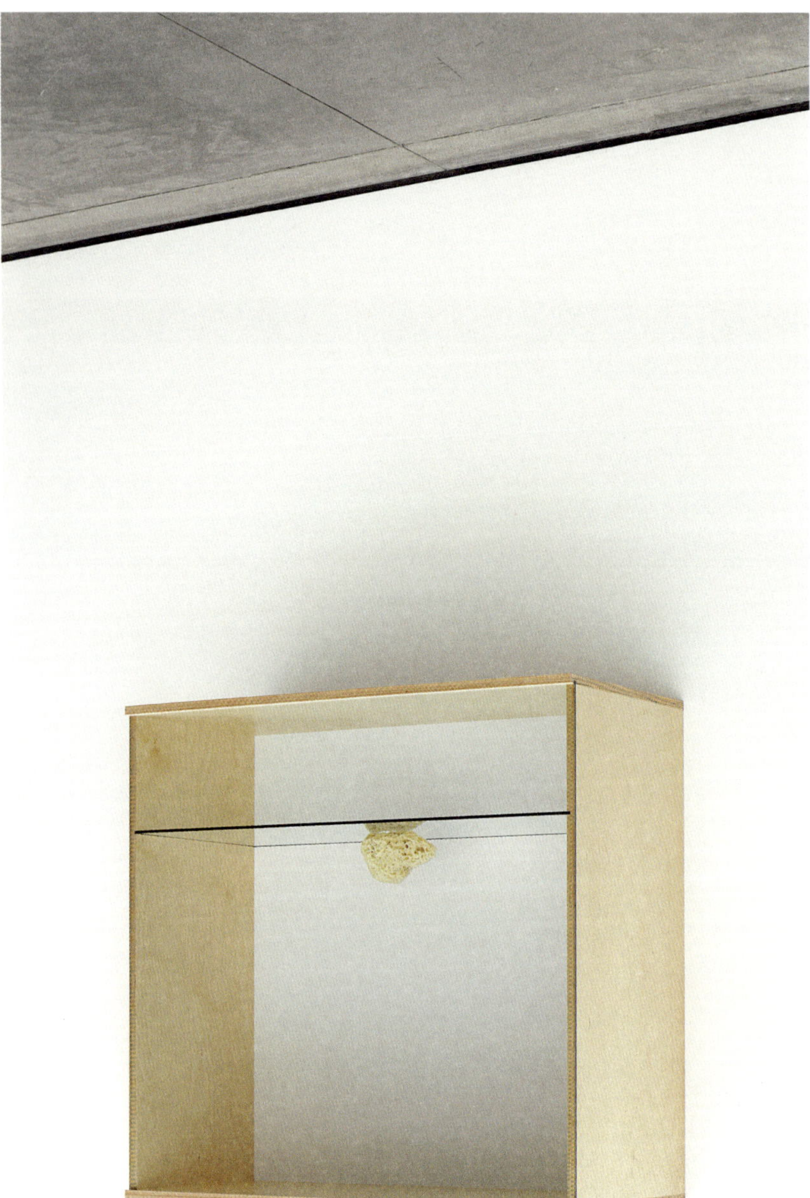

Your Castle In The Sky.

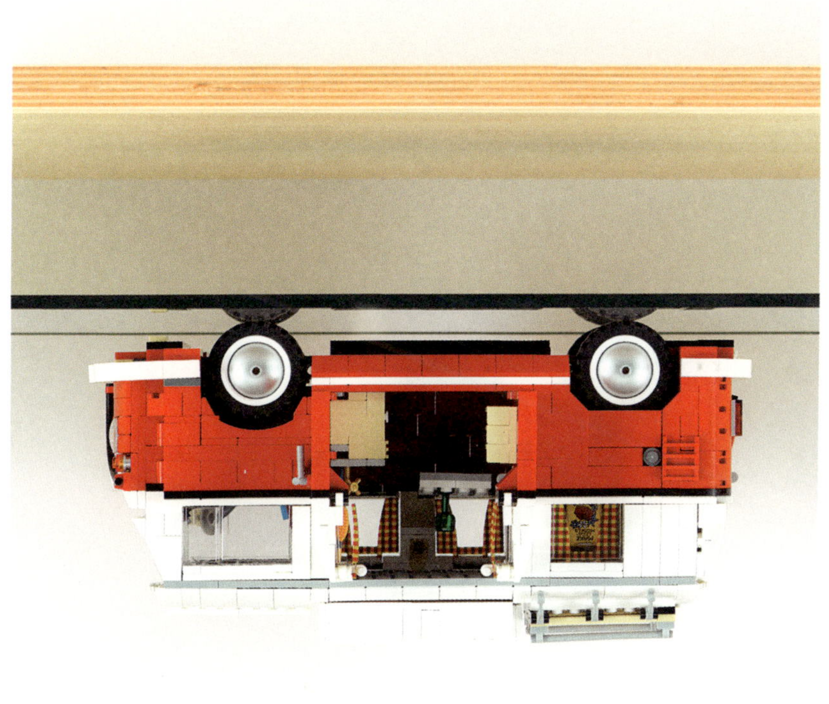

Somewhere in the twists and turns of a vexing debate could lie a new understanding of the universe, space and time — with suitably unpredictable consequences.

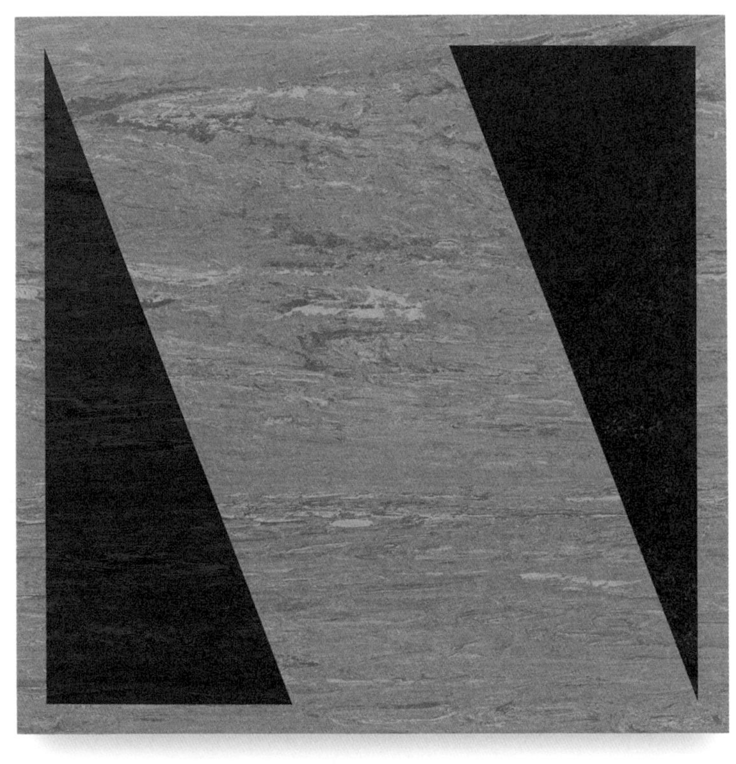

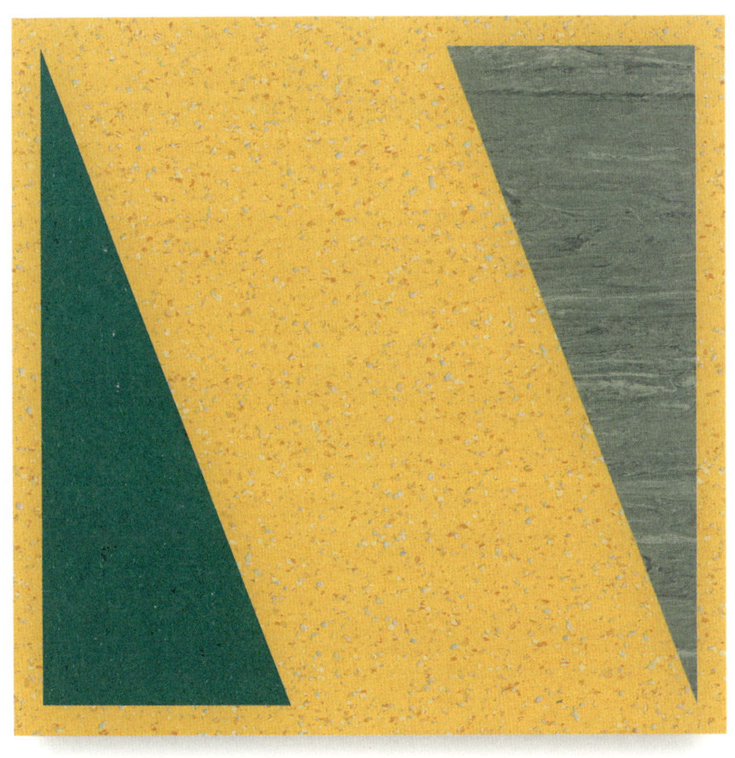

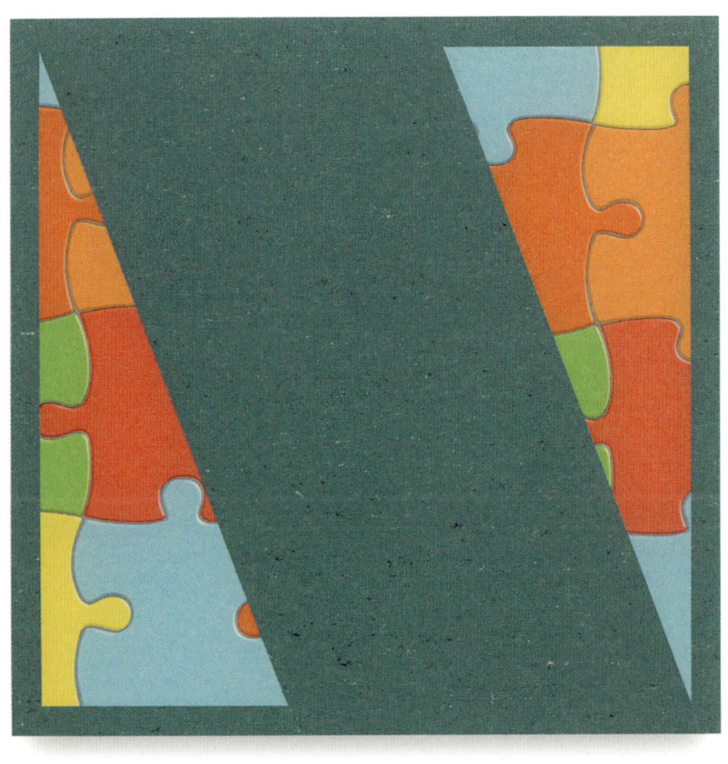

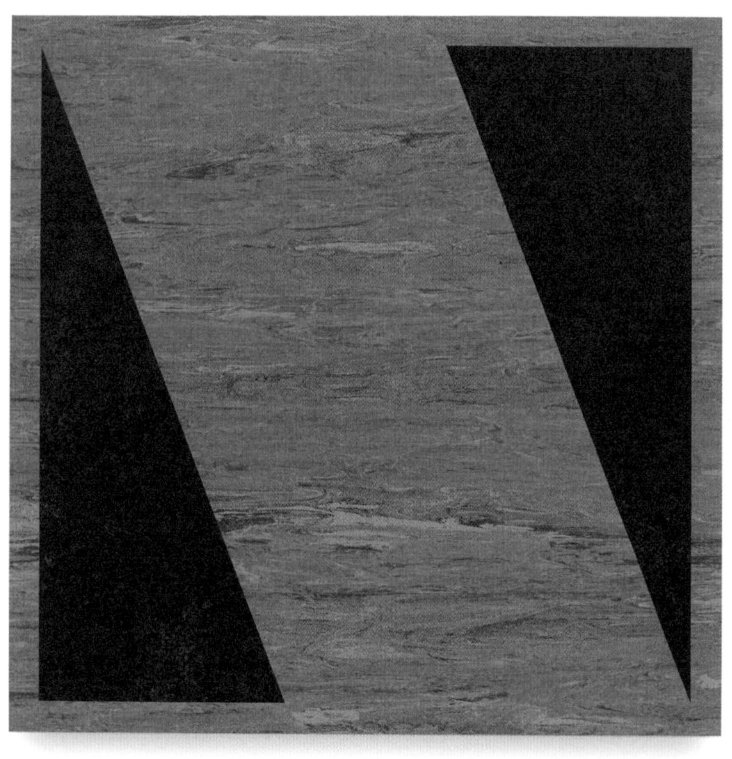

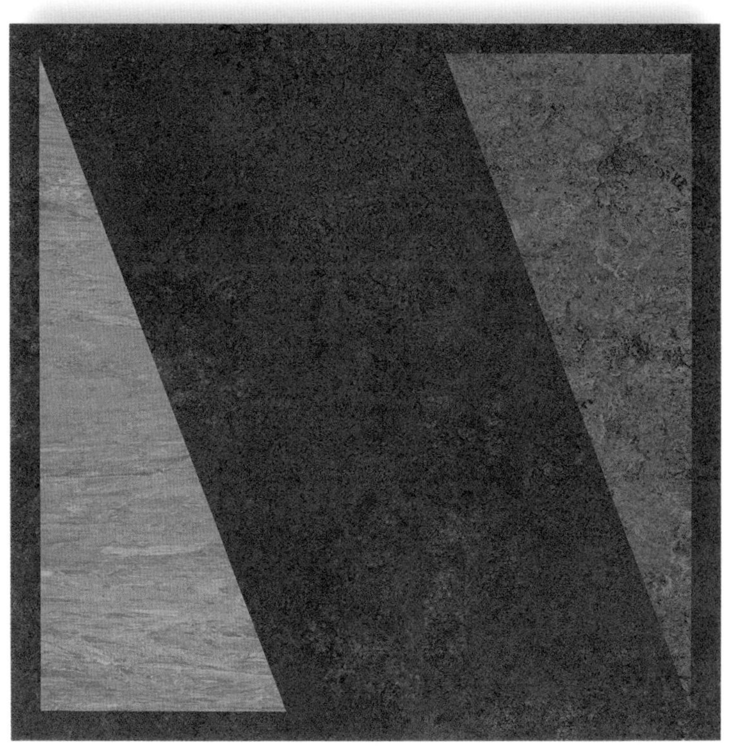

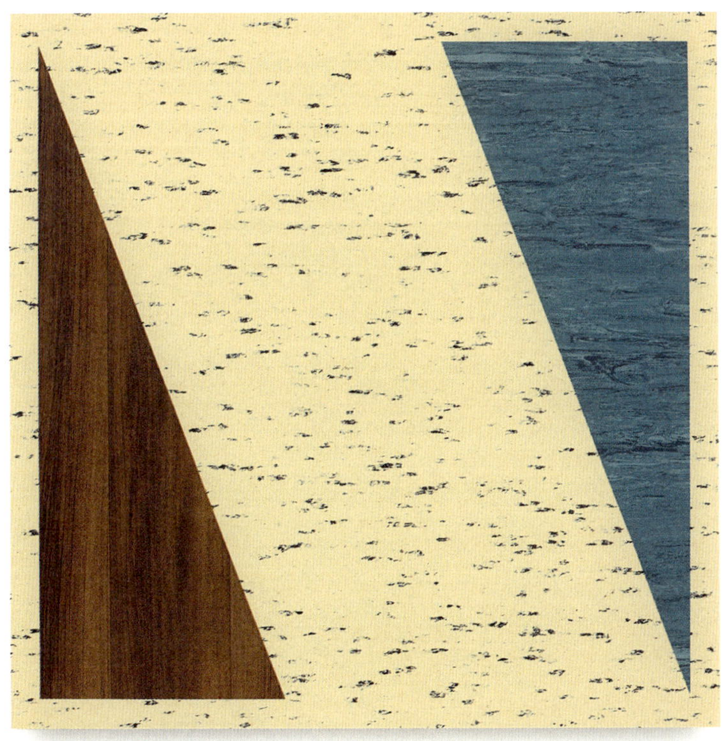

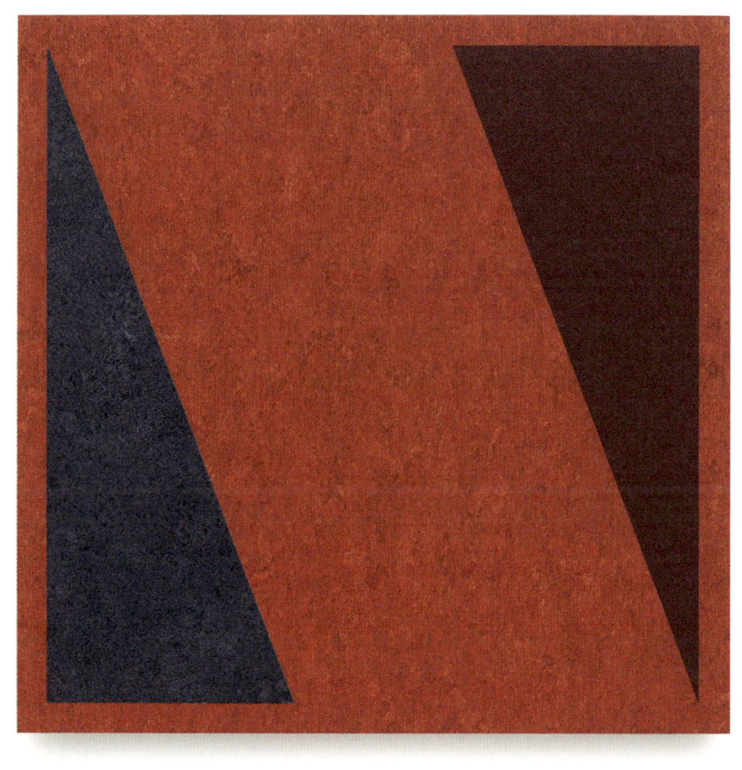

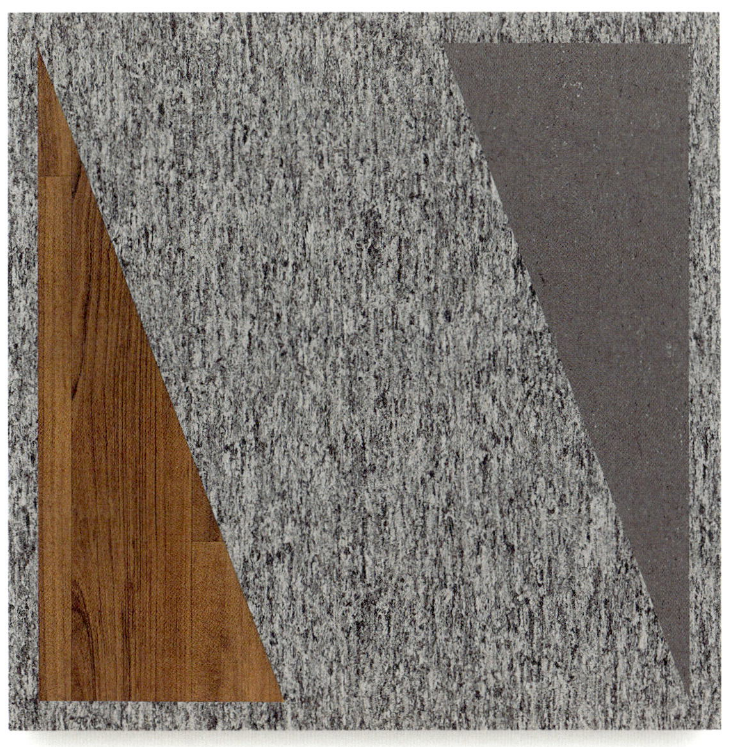

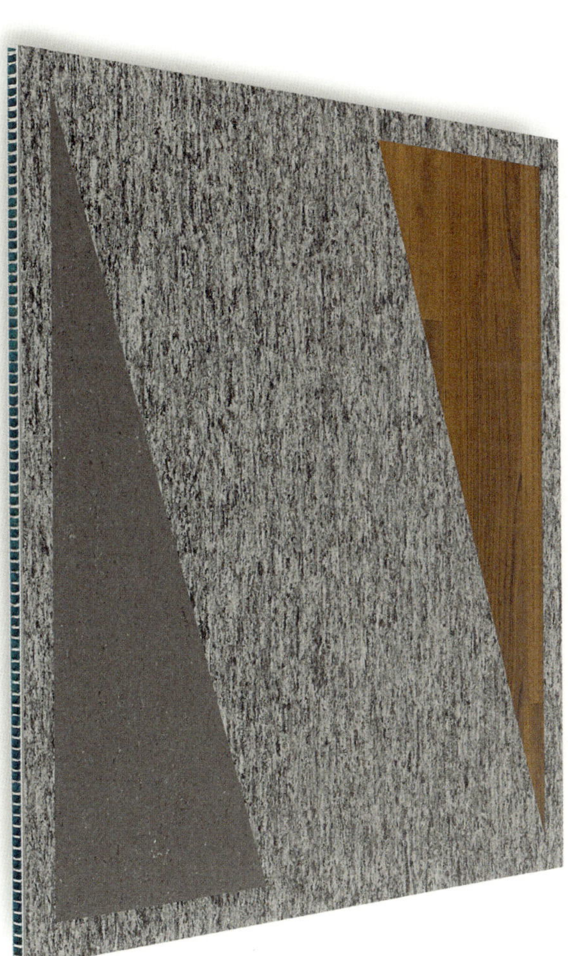

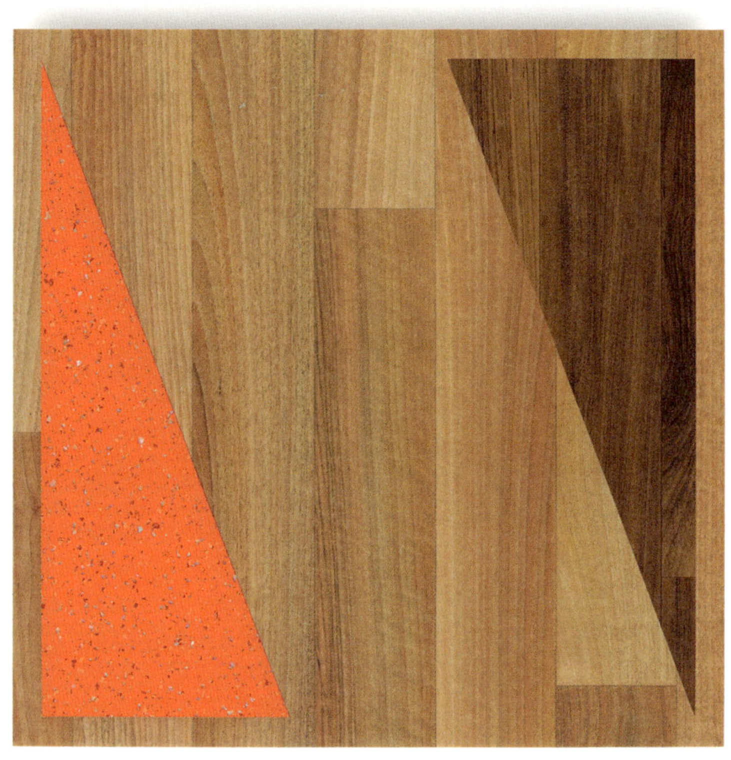

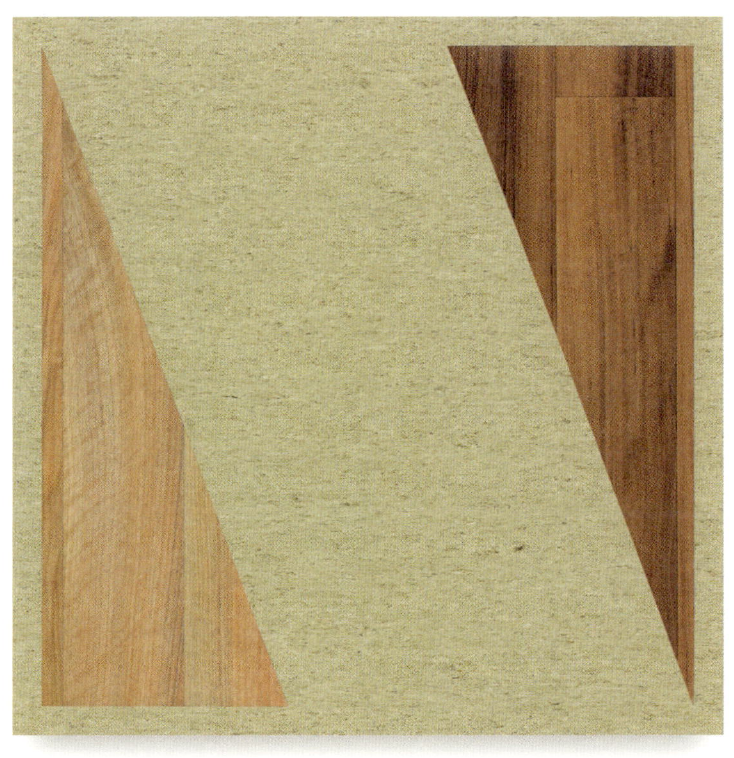

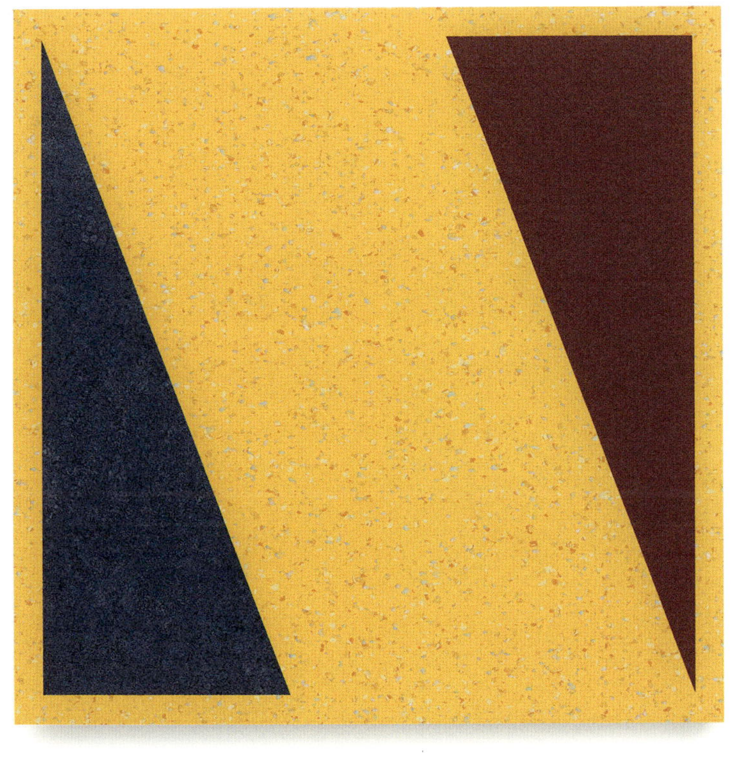

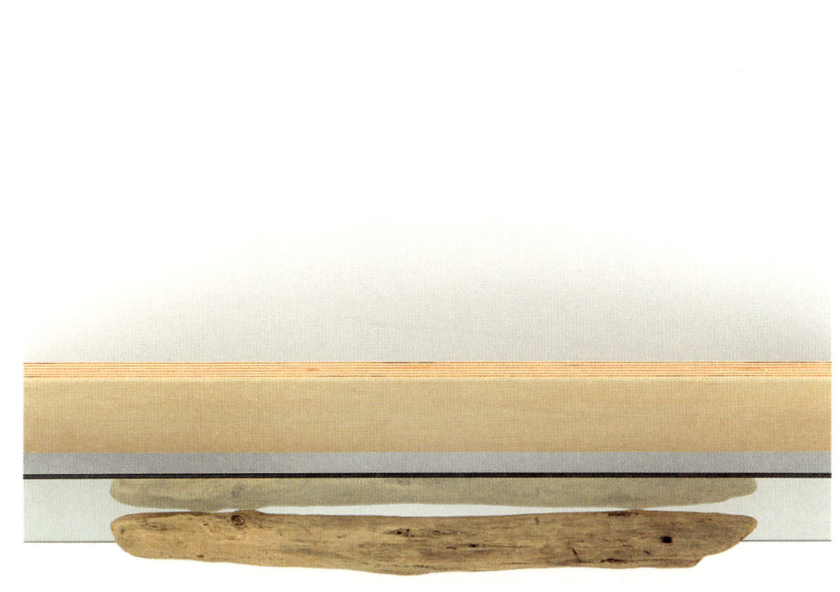

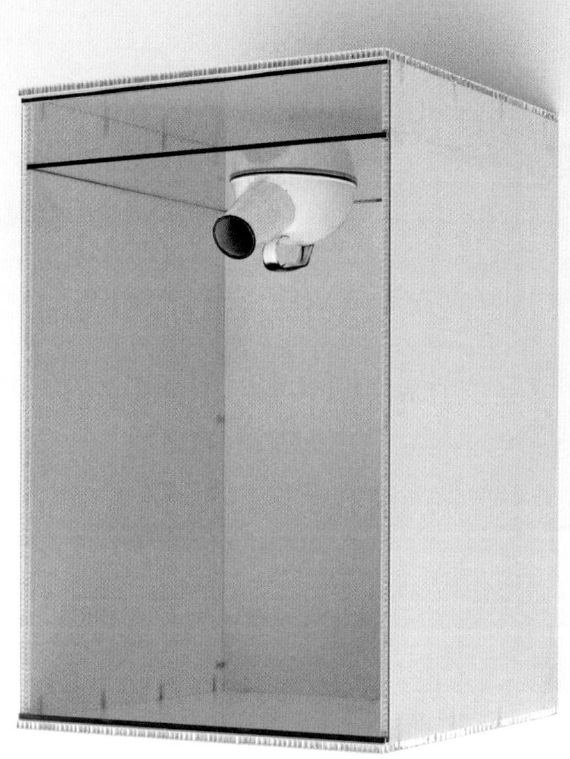

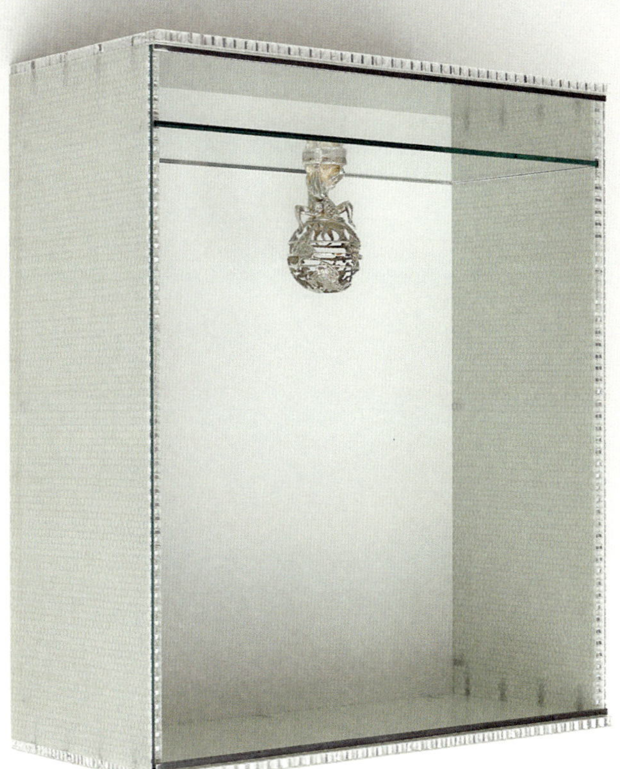

be late

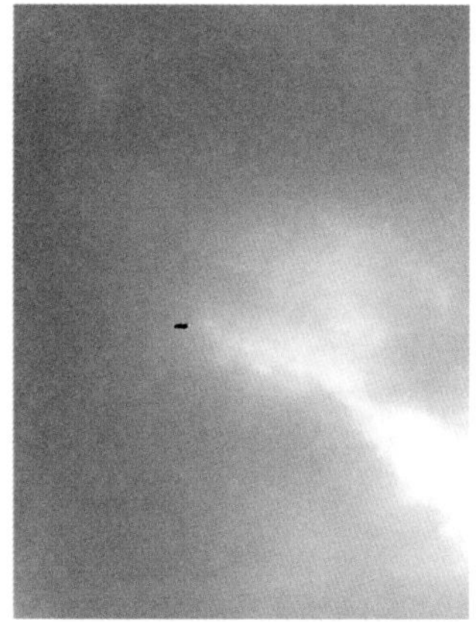

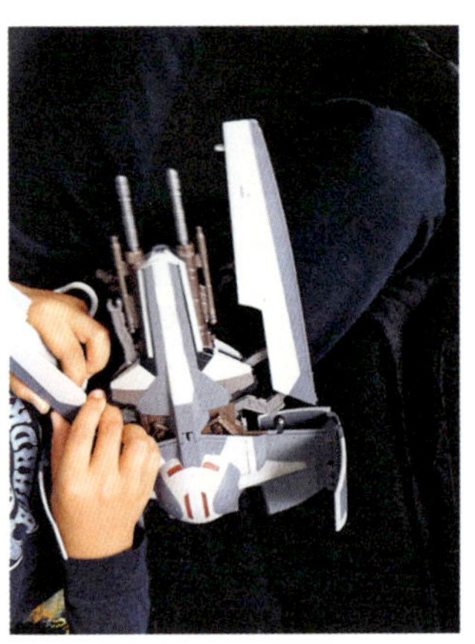

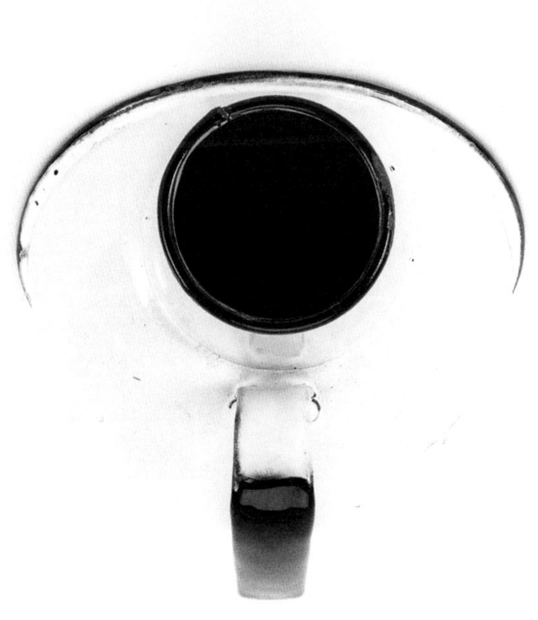

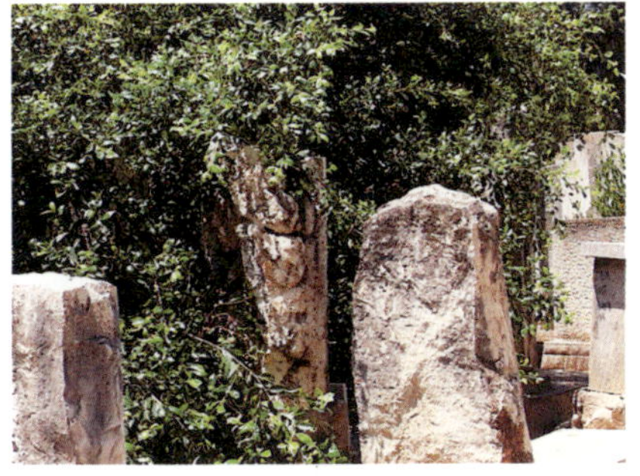

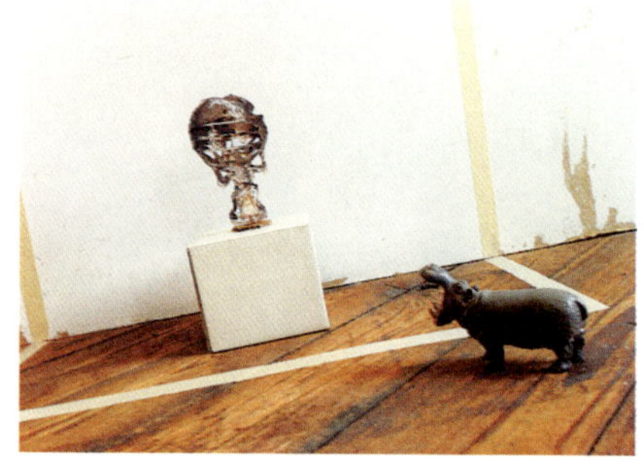

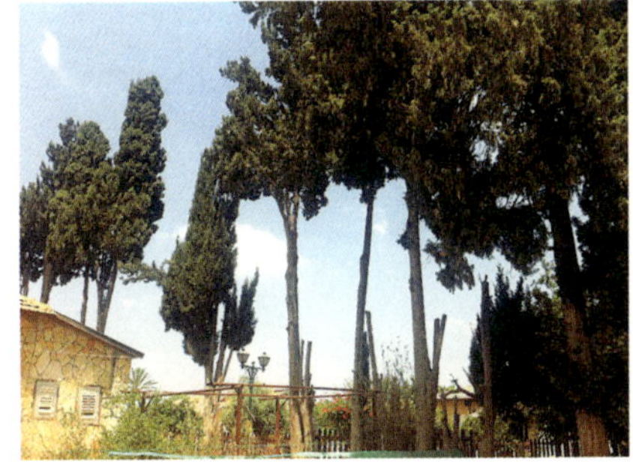

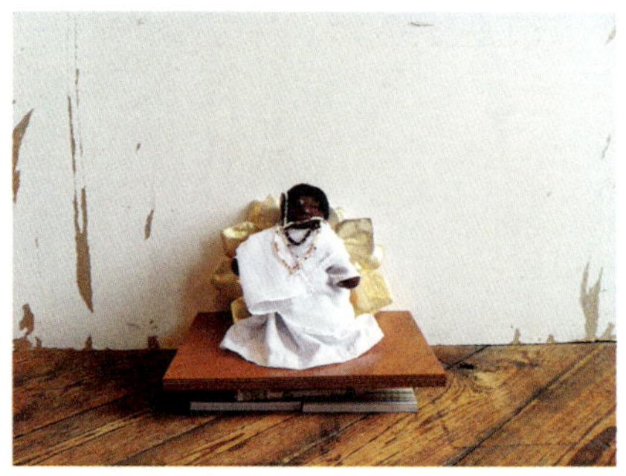

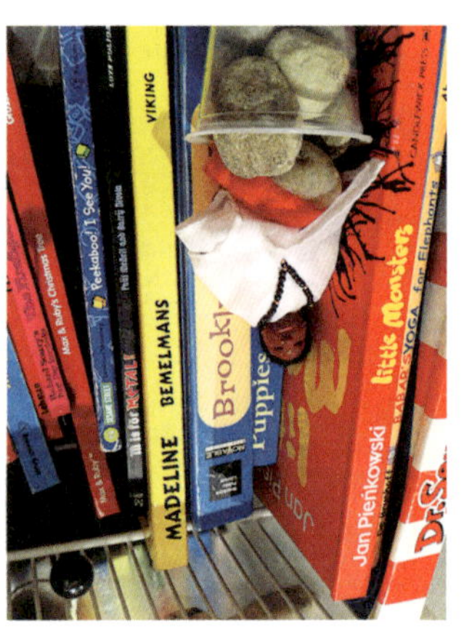

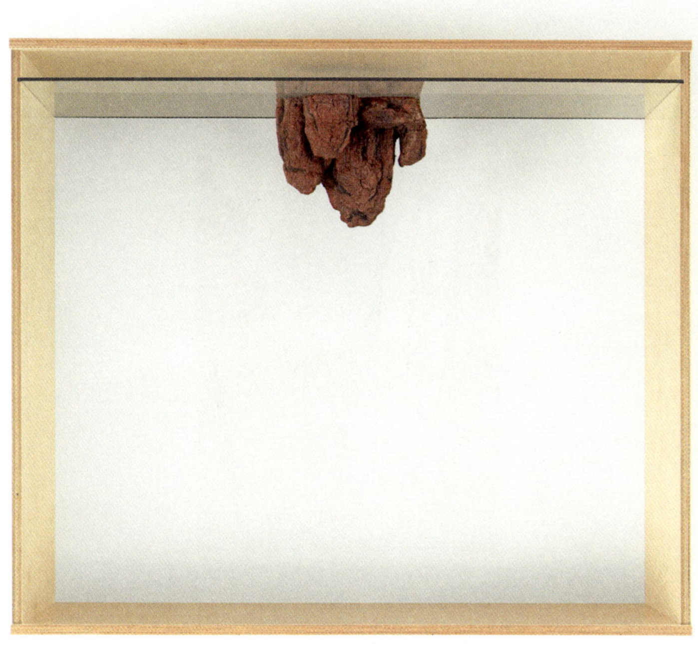

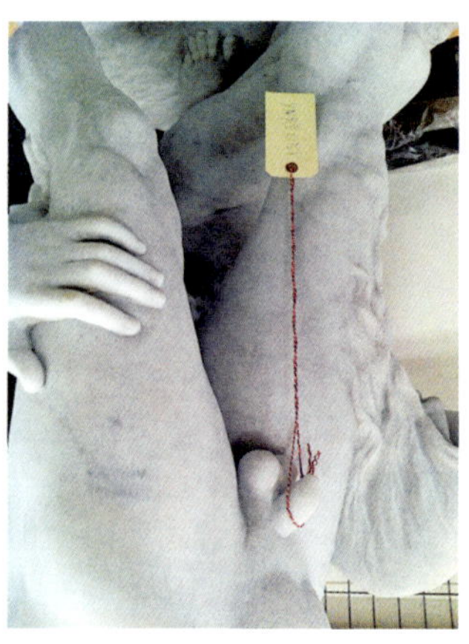

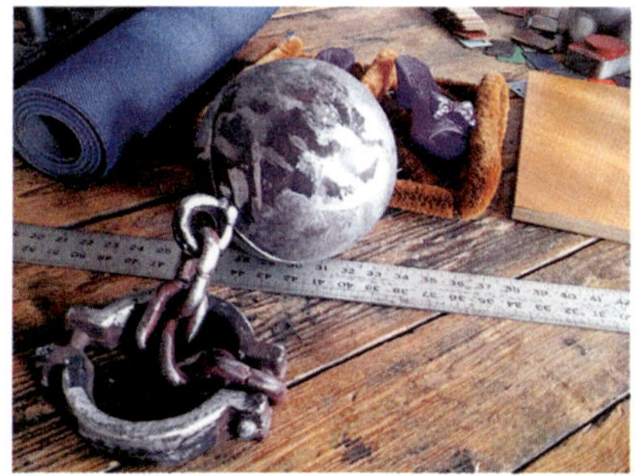

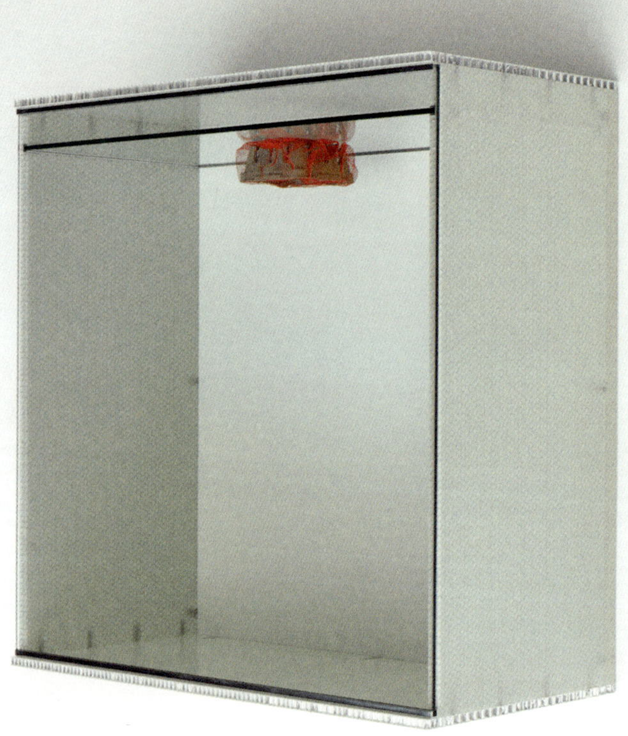

The difference between zoom and zoooooooooooooom.

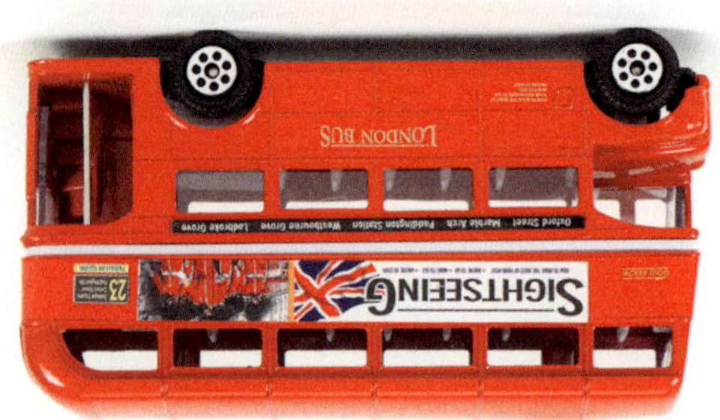
LONDON BUS
SIGHTSEEING
Oxford Street   Marble Arch   Paddington Station   Westbourne Grove   Ladbroke Grove
23

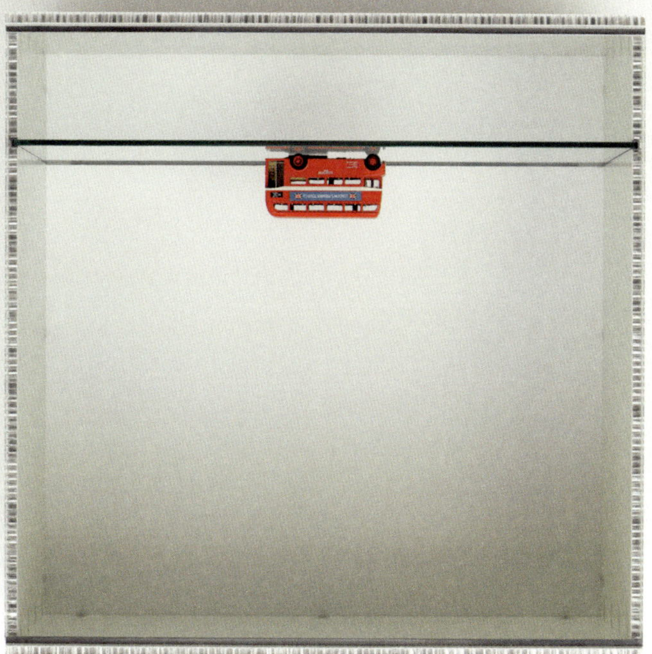

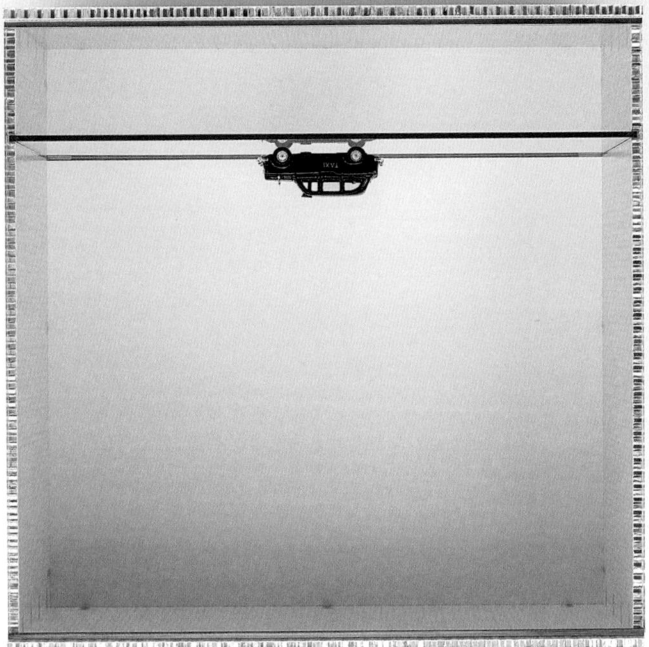

TAXI

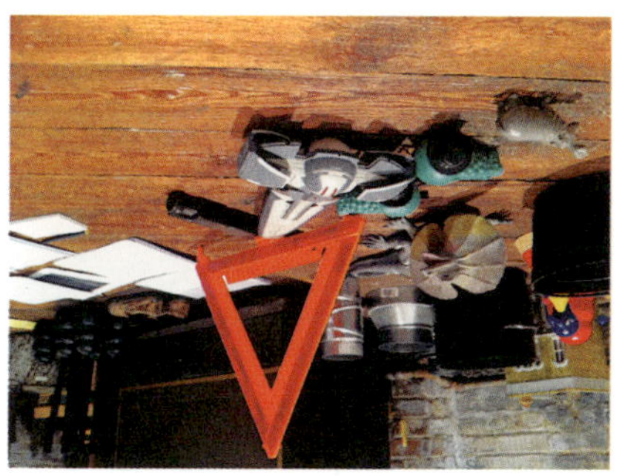

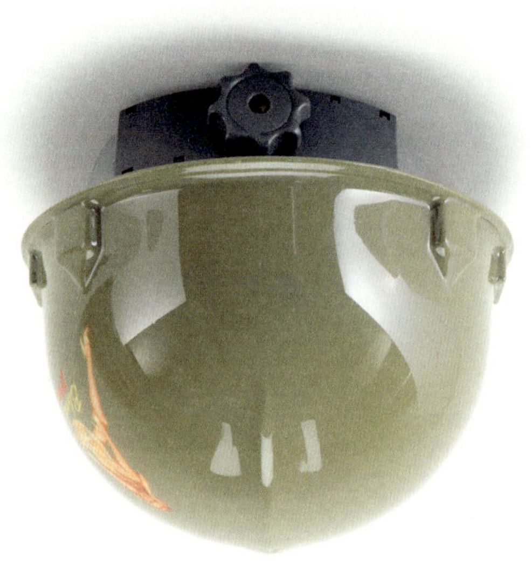

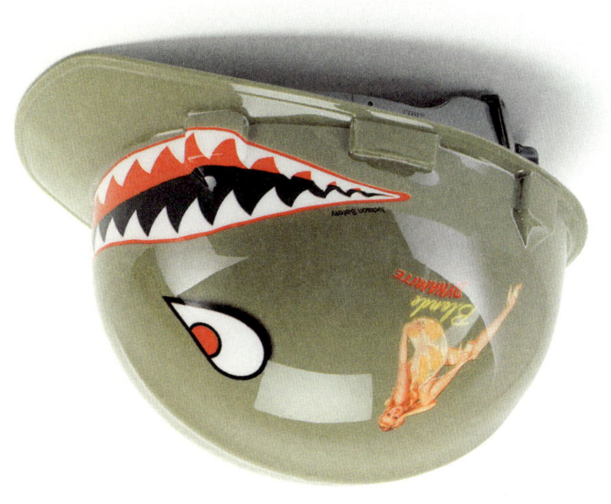
Blonde DYNAMITE

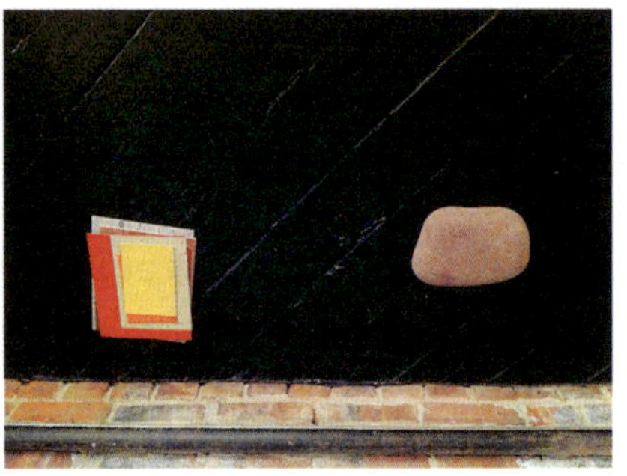

The Unstatic

Circulation

The *Porifera Demospongiae* is one of the oldest multicellular organisms on earth. Quite literally a body without organs, its whip-like flagella coax the ocean's tide through thousands of pores and channels and then up a jelly-filled chamber where it gathers nutrients. *Demospongiae* don't have built-in nervous or circulatory systems, so they rely on the continuous flow of water to animate and sustain their spongy frames. Scientists report that these ancient metazoans have given rise to some of the most diverse species on earth, forming the crucial link between single-cell choanoflagellates and more complex animals like horses and humans.

As the story of the sponge continues 580 million years down the line, its fibrous body reappears dried out on a beach, bleached in the sun's heat and harvested by its distant human ancestors. Over time, sponges became valued for how well they sloughed off dirt in a bath, handily cleaned unmentionable orifices, or aided contraception. The Romans used them as soft padding for armour, and in the Renaissance, they travelled to artists' studios, because they were the perfect texture for applying paints and glazes. In the late twentieth century, an American cartoon gave a sponge (named Bob) square pants, making it the stuff of legend.[1]

On a recent trip to London, Haim Steinbach found himself walking down the toiletries aisle of the department store Fortnum & Mason, when he noticed a sponge. He didn't buy it at first, but later the image of its honey-coloured body and porous irregularities returned to him. What an alien thing a sponge is when one thinks about it. A creature from the sea whose circulations have carried it from battle-gear to our bathtubs, whose travels through time give it life like the changing tide. His box gives this sponge back to us in all its strangeness, asking us to join its journey.

'Travel', the nomenclature Steinbach gives to his latest body of work, invites us to consider the way objects move materially and metonymically along a continuum. To map Steinbach's works is to see these objects as dynamic registrations of psychological, cultural, political, social and material shifts: ossifications and liquidations that, even after their initial selection and display, continue to inflect the valence an object has at any particular moment.

It may seem odd, at first, to consider Steinbach's works in the context of travel and movement, or within the framework of a processual dynamism. For we could make the mistake of thinking that his judicious structures predetermine meaning; that a found object is by definition a product; or that an object sitting silently on display is moribund, rather than waiting to dance with the tide like a jelly sponge.

A couple of points may help. The first is that Steinbach does not make sculptures. He makes arrangements on shelves. The second is that he works with everyday objects, not 'readymades'. These semantic distinctions, which the artist continuously makes in interviews, and the majority of his critics continue to overlook, are crucial for understanding what Steinbach hopes to offer us through his canny displays of ancient vessels, perfume bottles and silver statuettes. They are related, because in both cases Steinbach wants to keep us from getting too caught up in the genre of art or its canonised artspeak, where the 'readymade' reigns pre-eminent. Instead, he wants to show us how any piece of material culture — be it a piece of driftwood, a double-decker bus, a bocce ball — is constantly on the move, travelling from our bedrooms to our attics, and, if it's ever so lucky as to get into his hands, back into circulation riding the smooth glass ledge in a honeycomb panelled box.[2] Steinbach reminds us that an object can be art, but it plays other roles too.

Changing Displays

Getting to know Steinbach's games, a viewer discovers that sometimes the most insightful stories lie at the perimeters of the displays, in the interstitial space of something being on the shelf, and off it. (For example, Steinbach loves the thought of collectors cleaning his objects. Nothing is ever glued down, and so items can be dusted, rearranged, and even put to use.) His logic of the everyday asks us to take regular stuff just as seriously as we would art. To see what changes about a linoleum tile, for example, when it's hung on the wall like a painting. Two of the funniest examples of this everydayness embedded in his work involve outright theft. At one of Steinbach's first exhibitions, *Changing Displays*, at Fashion Moda in the South Bronx in 1980, his installation included a man's shirt hanging from a nail. A visitor who walked in from a methadone clinic next door saw it and, figuring he liked it better than his own, confidently exchanged his shirt with it and walked out. When showing *charm of tradition* (1985) at an upscale gallery in the late-1980s, a man came in to admire a pair of sparkling new high-tops sitting on a shelf. After asking the gallerist if the shoes were for sale ('No, don't touch. It's Art!'), he snatched them and disappeared.

Steinbach has changed other people's displays too. For his project for Documenta IX in 1992, he collaborated with its Artistic Director Jan Hoet, who generously offered him a sizeable collection of small items from his office. Steinbach made an elaborate display of the objects on a round tiered shelving unit, arranging the selections to great effect. When the exhibition was over, Hoet received his objects back, yet in an entirely new form. He purchased Steinbach's work for his museum, *Display #30 — An Offering (collectibles of Jan Hoet)*. In Steinbach's world, objects are never sterile or mute or over-determined, and they never come to a halt. Their paths are inherently twisted, shifting from one social valuation to another with the procession of time, neglect, or rediscovery. A thing may become a product, an artwork, and an heirloom all within one lifespan, and no matter how static an object may seem, its value as a thing is bound to the contingencies of its social life.

The Social Life of Things

In 1986, a few years after Steinbach first introduced his shelf displays of everyday objects, the anthropologist Arjun Appadurai edited a collection of essays titled *The Social Life of Things*. The book represented a significant methodological shift in the fields of anthropology, sociology and science studies, one that took into account the way the composition or significance of objects changes over time as they move from one cultural context to another and become embedded in new relations with other things. Appadurai was especially interested in how the term commodity could not sufficiently describe an object over the whole of its lifespan. He thought instead that it was merely one phase of a thing's social life, gaining or losing significance as it travelled through different regimes of value, in different social circles, as it aged and detached from a social whole. Not unlike the old adage, 'one man's trash is another man's treasure', this approach to objects attended to the ways they could communicate complex and context-dependent messages within a social framework.

To really understand a person or thing, one had to follow its pathways, or as Appadurai put it, 'it is the things-in-motion that illuminate their human and social context.'[3]

For all of this talk of movement, nonetheless, we face the very real problem that the object seems still to us, even directly given *as such* and not a sedimentation of previous travels. Apadurai addresses this stillness by describing objecthood as 'a momentary respite' for things whose properties are always in motion.[4] One may quibble about whether objects, or even images for that matter, can in fact be severed from their properties, or break out of duration for a rest. Yet there is a lot to gain in remembering that a thing bears the marks of its biography, and that these accumulations contain the potential to propel it elsewhere. In the same way that a photograph freezes a moment in time, concealing the durational quality of lived experience, objects too are *compressions* of an entire history of changing hands. Steinbach's arrangements make us sensitive to how an object's history is written on its surface and even how display itself has an enlivening capacity. His objects participate in a dense sociality, as he insists that we consider the story of an object's plastic, knotty, glossy, rough, shop-worn presence before us, which says something without so many words.

Object-Oriented

Today a number of thinkers are returning to the term 'object', and in some respects, are extending previous theories about its social lives to better account for its exchanges with *all* entitites in equal measure, not just how objects have meaning for humans. Sociologist Bruno Latour, for instance, has worked for many years to develop a theoretical position that sets humans and nonhumans on such a flat ontological plane. He seeks to account for relations between *things* (his substitute for 'objects'), a way of viewing the world as a network of socially inscribed events between *actants*, rather than an unknowable outside world at odds with the rational subject.

For Latour, the modernist divisions between subject and object don't apply, or as philosopher Graham Harman puts it: 'the isolated Kantian human is no more and no less an actor than are windmills, sunflowers, propane tanks, and Thailand.'[5] An important implication of this actor-network for Latour is that no one part of the system of relations can be reduced to another. Thus trying to understand the significance of windmills, for example, involves an entire chain of interwoven actant events, be they social, biological, technological and so on. Every 'thing' in the world is the result of numerous translations that have occurred over a series of things coming together. There is no unmediated existence, no 'pure' object, no 'facts' — just things.

Following Latour, the political theorist Jane Bennett argues for a 'vital materiality' that runs across a diverse assemblage of bodies, both physical and psychological, simple and complex.[6] She talks about a distributed agency of things, that doesn't see sociality as something unique to human language and culture, but as a driving force between objects of all kinds. Her 'political ecology of things' allows us to imagine how spinach pathogens, tornados and trash all make a difference: ordinary things forming collectives, exerting pressure on certain trajectories, and having a powerful influence on how we live (and what makes 'us' up). Harman's object-oriented philosophy thinks about objects in a similar way, wanting to do away with the primacy of human perception. He extends this sensual capacity — and its limitations — to all things: trains, babies, Coca-Cola, and the tooth fairy are all objects, and they sense the world in their own train, baby, Coca-Cola, and tooth fairy ways. Yet importantly for Harman, none of these objects is ever exhausted by its relations with other things. An object always withdraws into its object-being, sharing itself indirectly through translation, yet never showing itself for what it is in all its fullness.

Circulation

One way of looking at an object's travels today, then, is to acknowledge its interactions with human, nonhuman, natural, and artificial entities alike. From this perspective, Steinbach's objects are not merely invested in the way that the signification of objects shifts between contexts — an interest shared by many artists using appropriative strategies — but also in the accretions and embedded histories of culture wrought in the material surfaces and shapes of things themselves. In other words, Steinbach cares *both* about how cultural valuation gets altered through language and how the stuff of everyday life has its own rich material interchange in excess of what might be said about it by us. Pushing this a bit further, we can understand his works as invested equally in revealing how objects gain or lose different kinds of significance for humans (a piece of junk becomes a family heirloom becomes valuable as art), but that they are at the same time undeniably concrete material aggregations of a human-inhuman matrix that continue to gather momentum as they take on new forms over time. A choanoflagellate becomes a *Demospongiae* becomes a Roman who uses a sponge.

Jenny Jaskey

Notes

1
'SpongeBob SquarePants' is a popular animated television series created by marine biologist Stephen Hillenburg. It follows the adventures of a bright yellow sponge in the underwater city of Bikini Bottom.

2
The artist's most recent displays are fabricated from fibreglass-faced honeycomb boards used in airplane construction.

3
Appadurai, Arjun. 'Commodities and the Politics of Value', *The Social Lives of Things: Commodities in Cultural Perspective* (Cambridge: Cambridge University Press, 1986), p. 5.

4
'In some way, all things are congealed moments in a longer social trajectory. All things are brief deposits of this or that property, photographs that conceal the reality of the motion from which their objecthood is a momentary respite.' Appadurai, Arjun, 'The Thing Itself', *Public Culture* 18.1 (Durham: Duke University Press, 2006), pp. 15–21.

5
Harman, Graham. *Prince of Networks: Bruno Latour and Metaphysics* (Melbourne: re.press, 2009), p. 14.

6
Bennett, Jane. *Vibrant Matter: A Political Economy of Things* (Durham: Duke University Press, 2010).

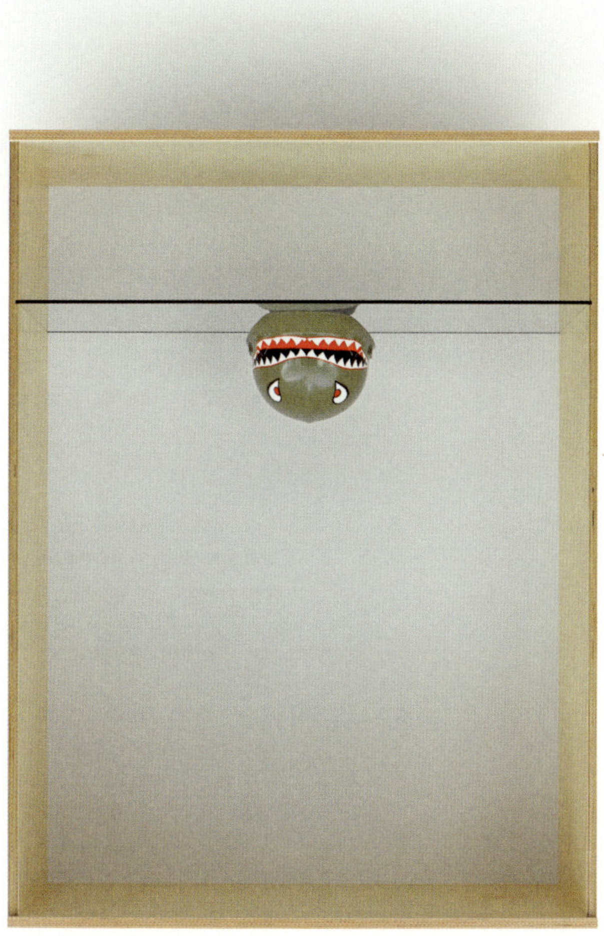

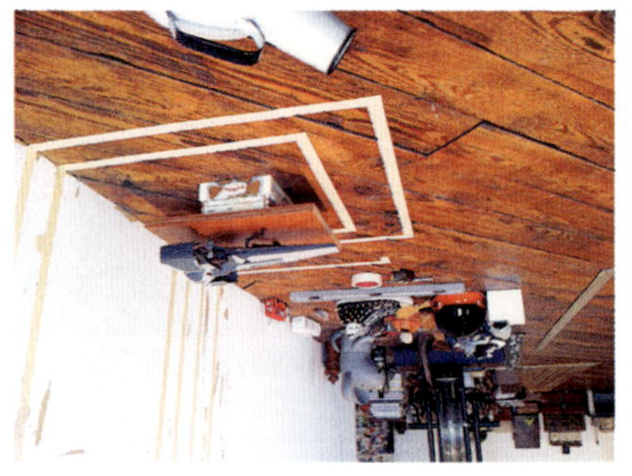

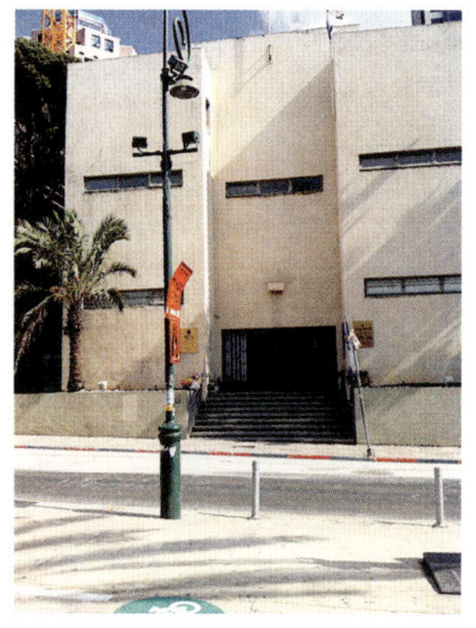

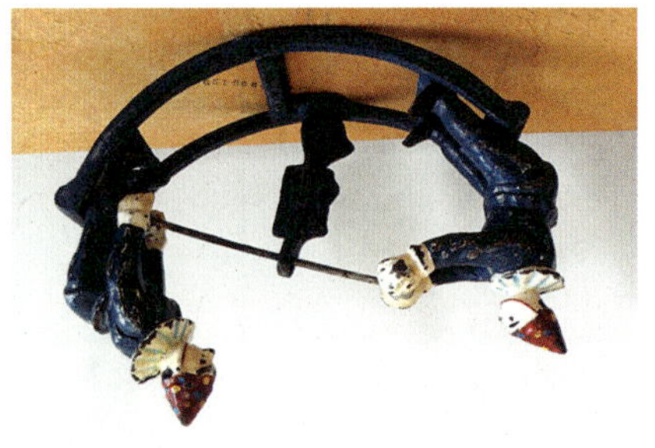

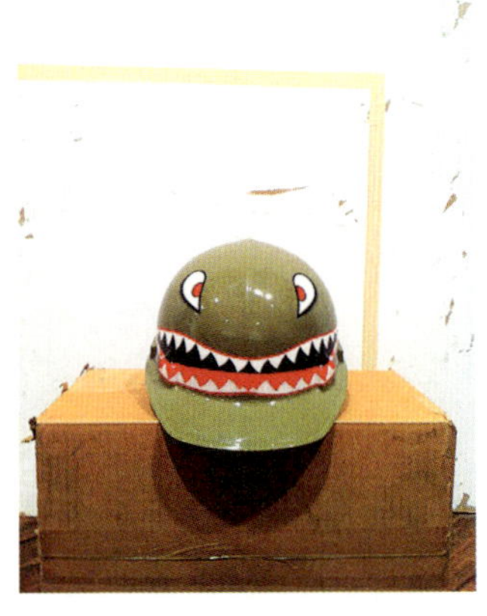

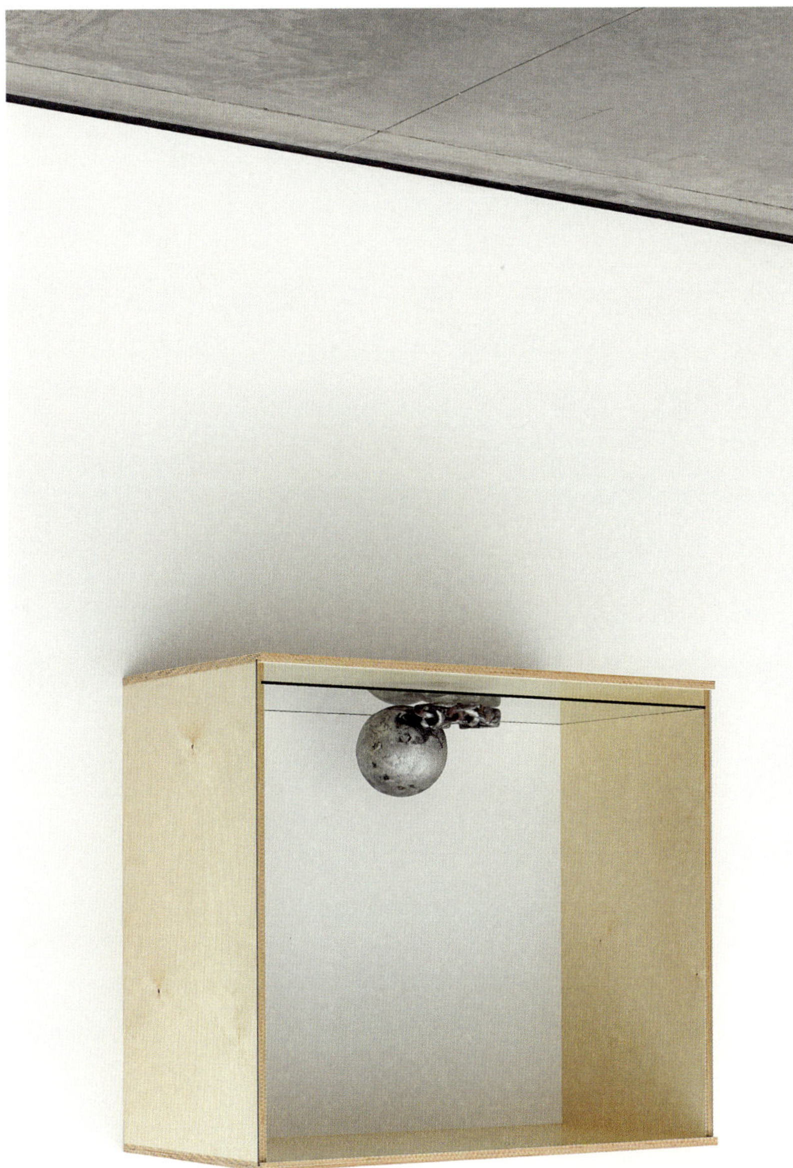

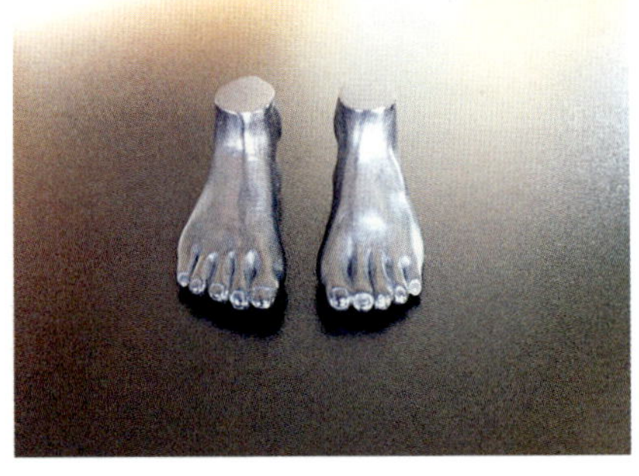

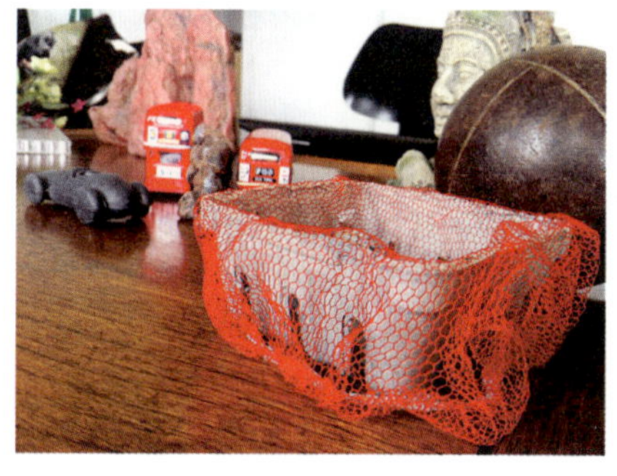

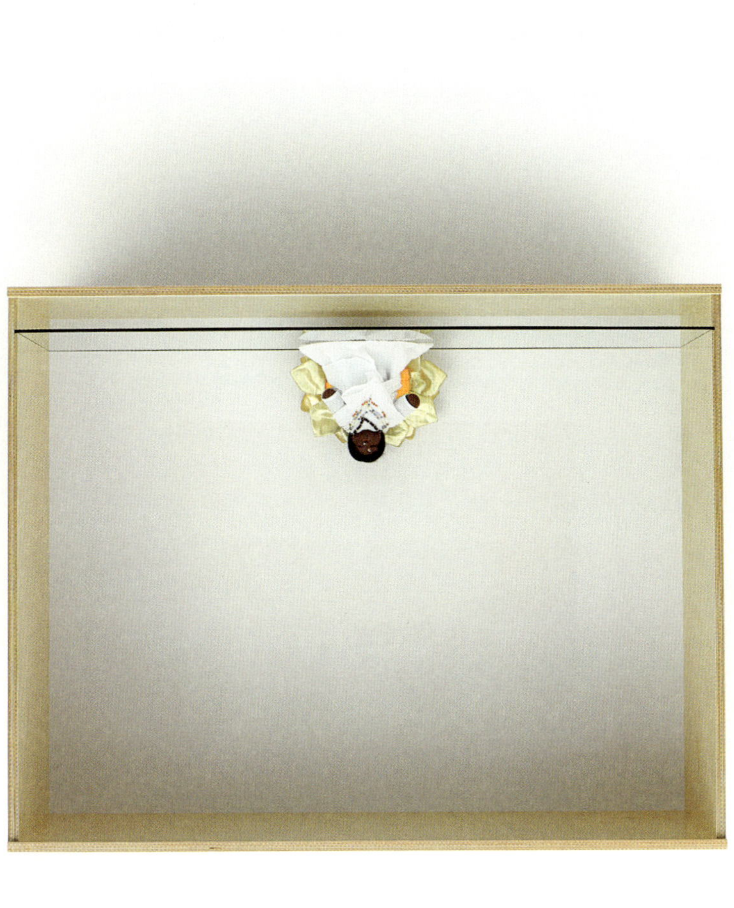

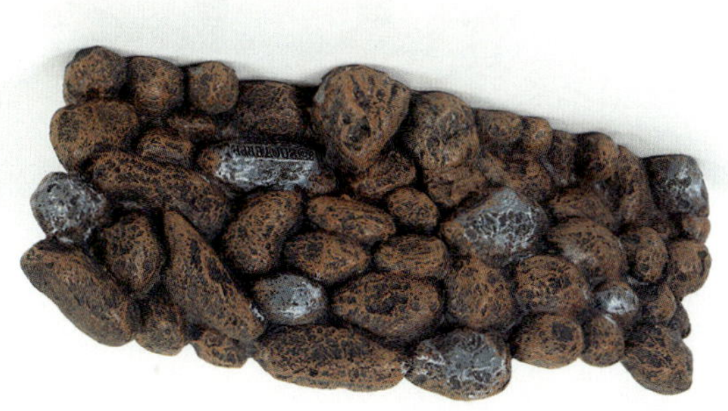

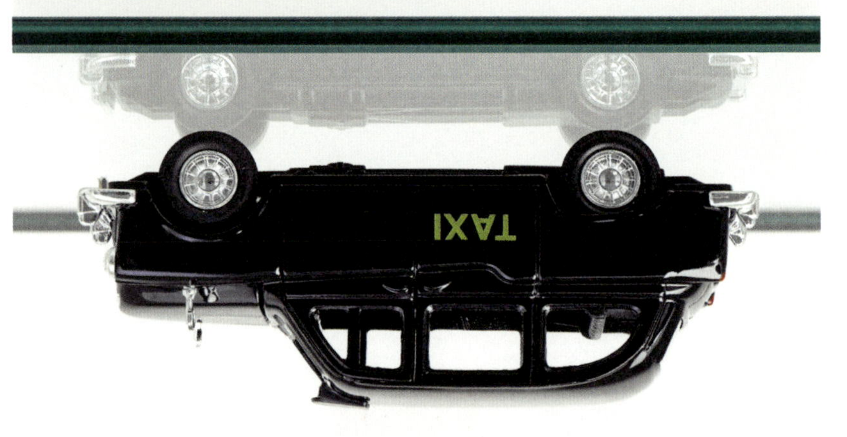

TAXI

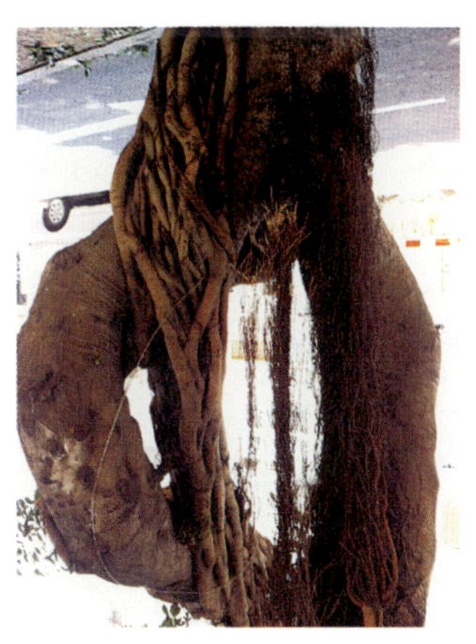

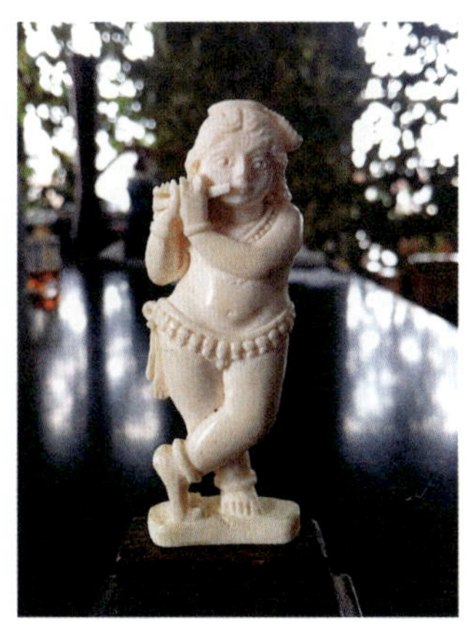

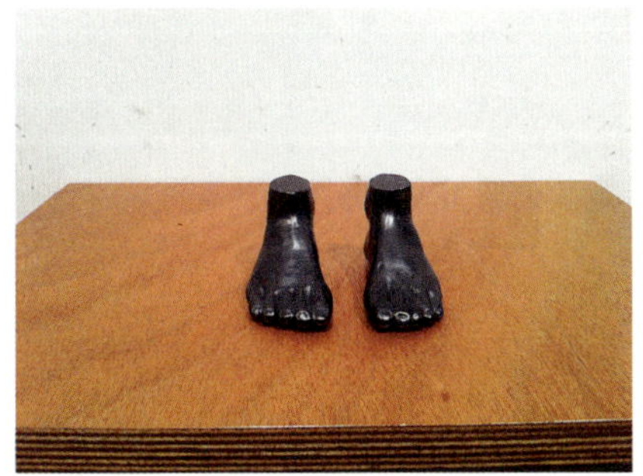

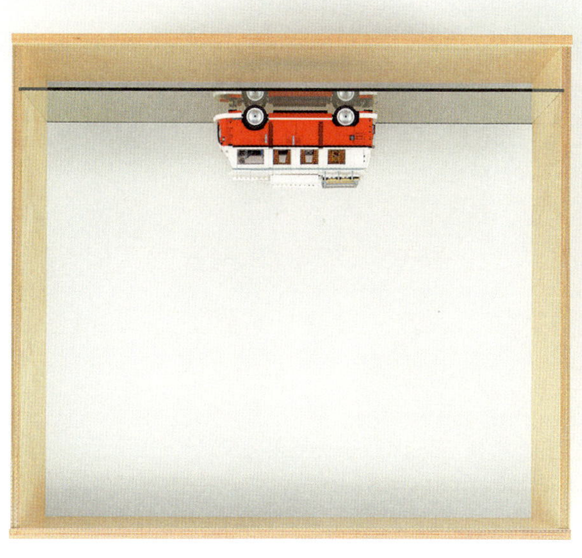

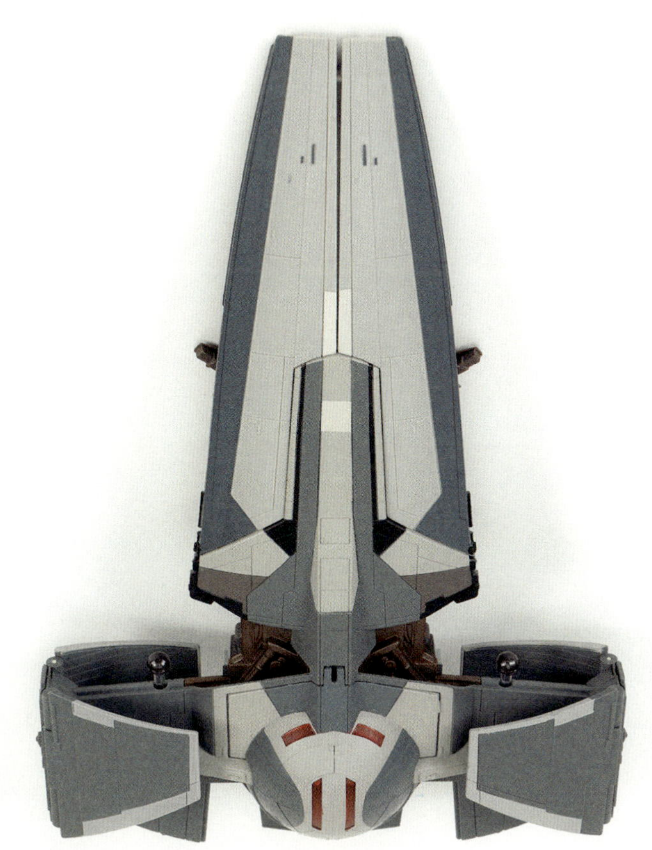

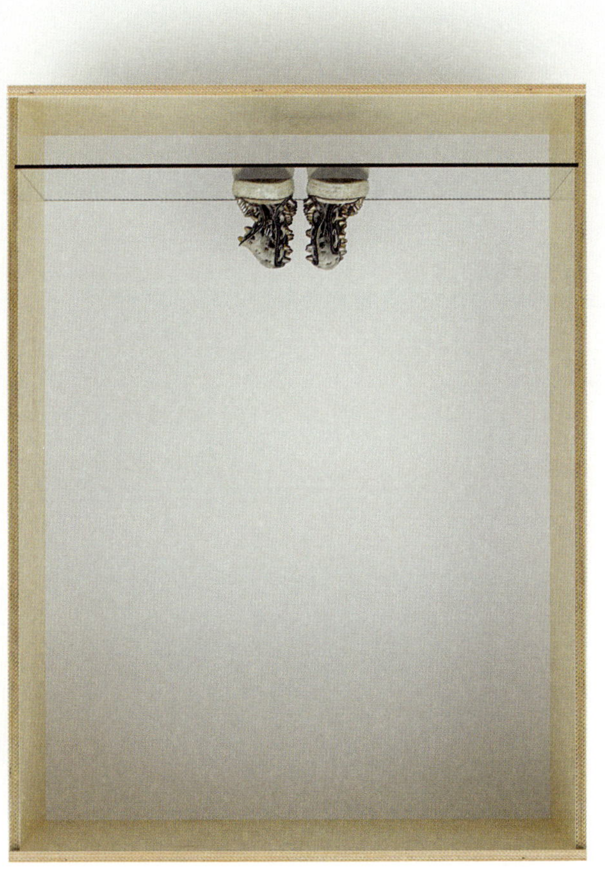

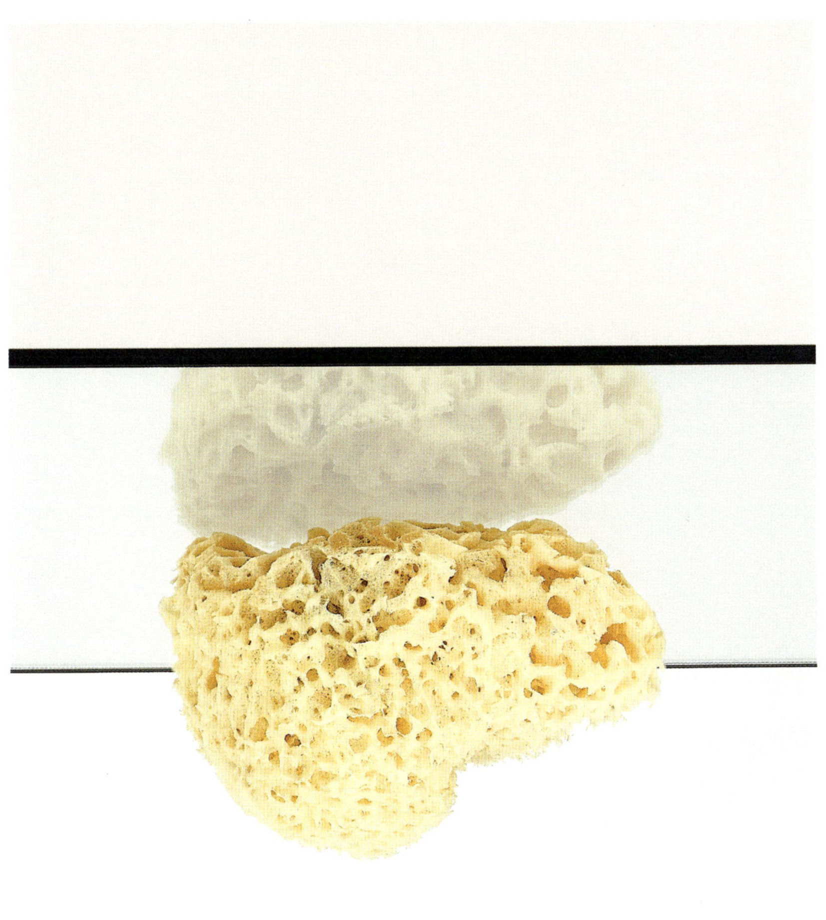

Going

going

gone.

Haim Steinbach

Haim Steinbach was born in 1944 in Rehovot, Israel, and lives and works in New York. He received a BFA from Pratt Institute, New York in 1968 and an MFA from Yale University, New Haven in 1973.

Steinbach has held solo exhibitions at CCS Bard Hessel Museum of Art, Annandale-on-Hudson, USA (2013); The Artist's Institute, New York (2012); Haus der Kunst, Munich (2000); Museum Moderner Kunst Stiftung Ludwig, Vienna (1997); Castello di Rivoli, Turin (1995); Solomon R. Guggenheim Museum, New York (1993); Witte de With, Centre for Contemporary Art, Rotterdam (1992); CAPC musée d'art contemporain, Bordeaux (1988) and Artists Space, New York (1979).

His work has been included in group exhibitions at the Stedelijk Museum, Amsterdam (2012); Palais de Tokyo, Paris (2012); Museum of Contemporary Art, Montreal (2012); The Rubell Family Collection, Miami (2011); Peggy Guggenheim Collection, Venice (2011); Victoria and Albert Museum, London (2011); Hammer Museum, Los Angeles (2011); Museum of Contemporary Art Chicago (2010); Museum of Contemporary Art, Lyon (2009); S.M.A.K., Ghent (2008); Serpentine Gallery, London (2006); Museum für Gegenwartskunst, Basel (2005); New Museum of Contemporary Art, New York (2004); Tate Liverpool (2002); Centre George Pompidou, Paris (1990) and the Institute of Contemporary Art, Boston (1988).

His work was included in Documenta IX and the Sydney Biennial in 1992, the 1993 and 1997 Venice Biennales, the 2000 Biennale de Lyon, and La Triennale, Paris, in 2012.

List of works

pp. 7, 55
Untitled (Atlas)
2013
Fibreglass-faced honeycomb
boards, plastic laminate and
glass box; silver sculpture
26 ⁷⁄₈ × 22 ⁷⁄₈ × 10 ⁵⁄₈ in.
(68.1 × 58.1 × 26.9 cm)

p. 25
Untitled (perfume bottle)
2013
Fibreglass-faced honeycomb
boards, plastic laminate and
glass box; Chanel glass perfume
bottle
22 ⁷⁄₈ × 14 ⁷⁄₈ × 7 ¹⁄₂ in.
(57.9 × 37.6 × 19 cm)

pp. 26, 117
Untitled (sponge)
2013
Baltic birch plywood, plastic
laminate and glass box; natural
honeycomb sea sponge
37 ³⁄₈ × 38 ³⁄₈ × 18 ¹⁄₂ in.
(94.9 × 97.5 × 47 cm)

p. 31, 111
Untitled (camper)
2013
Baltic birch plywood, plastic
laminate and glass box; Lego
Volkswagen camper van
33 ³⁄₈ × 37 ³⁄₈ × 18 ¹⁄₂ in.
(84.8 × 94.9 × 47 cm)

p. 35
LP (d) 9/14/2013
2013
Linoleum, aluminium-faced
honeycomb board
23 ¹⁄₄ × 23 ¹⁄₄ × 1 ²⁄₈ in.
(59 × 59 × 2.7 cm)

p. 36
LP (b) 9/12/2013
2013
Linoleum, aluminium-faced
honeycomb board
23 ¹⁄₄ × 23 ¹⁄₄ × 1 ²⁄₈ in.
(59 × 59 × 2.7 cm)

p. 37
LP (b) 9/6/2013
2013
Linoleum, aluminium-faced
honeycomb board
23 ¹⁄₄ × 23 ¹⁄₄ × 1 ²⁄₈ in.
(59 × 59 × 2.7 cm)

p. 38
LP (f) 9/6/2013
2013
Linoleum, aluminium-faced
honeycomb board
23 ¹⁄₄ × 23 ¹⁄₄ × 1 ²⁄₈ in.
(59 × 59 × 2.7 cm)

p. 39
LP (c) 9/6/2013
2013
Linoleum, aluminium-faced
honeycomb board
23 ¹⁄₄ × 23 ¹⁄₄ × 1 ²⁄₈ in.
(59 × 59 × 2.7 cm)

p. 40
LP (d) 9/6/2013
2013
Linoleum, aluminium-faced
honeycomb board
23 ¼ × 23 ¼ × 1 ⅛ in.
(59 × 59 × 2.7 cm)

p. 41
LP (b) 9/3/2013
2013
Linoleum, aluminium-faced
honeycomb board
23 ¼ × 23 ¼ × 1 ⅛ in.
(59 × 59 × 2.7 cm)

p. 42
LP (a) 9/12/2013
2013
Linoleum, aluminium-faced
honeycomb board
23 ¼ × 23 ¼ × 1 ⅛ in.
(59 × 59 × 2.7 cm)

p. 43
LP (a) 9/3/2013
2013
Linoleum, aluminium-faced
honeycomb board
23 ¼ × 23 ¼ × 1 ⅛ in.
(59 × 59 × 2.7 cm)

p. 44, 45
LP (b) 9/23/2013
2013
Linoleum, aluminium-faced
honeycomb board
23 ¼ × 23 ¼ × 1 ⅛ in.
(59 × 59 × 2.7 cm)

p. 46
LP (a) 9/14/2013
2013
Linoleum, aluminium-faced
honeycomb board
23 ¼ × 23 ¼ × 1 ⅛ in.
(59 × 59 × 2.7 cm)

p. 47
LP (c) 9/14/2013
2013
Linoleum, aluminium-faced
honeycomb board
23 ¼ × 23 ¼ × 1 ⅛ in.
(59 × 59 × 2.7 cm)

p. 49
LP 9/5/2013
2013
Linoleum, aluminium-faced
honeycomb board
23 ¼ × 23 ¼ × 1 ⅛ in.
(59 × 59 × 2.7 cm)

p. 51
Untitled (driftwood)
2013
Baltic birch plywood, plastic
laminate and glass box;
driftwood
41 ⅜ × 55 ⅜ × 21 ½ in.
(105.1 × 145.7 × 54.6 cm)

p. 99
Untitled (ball & chain)
2013
Baltic birch plywood, plastic
laminate and glass box; plastic
ball and chain
$36\,^3/_8 \times 41\,^3/_8 \times 21\,^1/_2$ in.
(92.4 × 105.1 × 54.6 cm)

p. 103
Untitled (Amma)
2013
Baltic birch plywood, plastic
laminate and glass box; cotton,
polyester and plastic doll
(Amma)
$38\,^7/_8 \times 49\,^7/_8 \times 21\,^1/_2$ in.
(98.8 × 126.7 × 54.6 cm)

p. 115
Untitled (black sneakers)
2013
Baltic birch plywood, plastic
laminate and glass box; canvas,
rubber, metal 'Dirty Black
Sneakers' by Douglas Abraham
$48\,^3/_8 \times 36\,^3/_8 \times 21$ in.
(123 × 92.5 × 53.4 cm)

Haim Steinbach
Travel
2 October – 16 November 2013
White Cube Mason's Yard

Editor and Coordinator, Honey Luard
Assistant Editor, Robin Kirsten
Design, James Langdon
Print, MM Artbook printing & repro

Artworks © Haim Steinbach
Text © Jenny Jaskey
Catalogue © White Cube

Photography by Christopher Burke, Jack Hems, Haim Steinbach
and Benjamin Westoby.

Jenny Jaskey is curator of The Artist's Institute, New York.
Her favourite object is a paper weight in the shape of a golf ball.

978 1 906072 83 4

White Cube
25–26 Mason's Yard
St James's
London SW1Y 6BU

+44 (0)20 7930 5373
whitecube.com

Once again the world is flat.

Acknowledgements

Haim Steinbach would like to thank the following people for their invaluable contribution in the making of this publication, the exhibition and the new works for *Travel* at White Cube:

David Baker
David Board
Tanya Bonakdar
Céline Condorelli
Clare Coombes
Mark Darbyshire
Andrew Gwilliams
Lisa Hamilton
Ieuan Hemlock
Pete Howell
Vicky Jiang
Jay Jopling
Zerek Kempf
Robin Kirsten
James Langdon
Frances Loeffler
Honey Luard
Rose Marcus
Scott Martin
Susan May
Ellie Nicholls
David Northedge
John Silberman
Gwen Smith
River Steinbach
Joe Winter